C.B.S.E.
ARABIC
GRAMMAR

C.B.S.E.
ARABIC
GRAMMAR

Amanulla Vadakkangara

GOODWORD
www.goodwordbooks.com

Goodword Books Pvt. Ltd.
1, Nizamuddin West Market, New Delhi - 110 013
email: info@goodwordbooks.com
First published 2006
Reprinted 2010
© Goodword Books 2010
Printed in India

www.goodwordbooks.com

CONTENTS

ABOUT THE AUTHOR

Amanulla Vadakkangara was born in Vadakkangara, a village in Malappuram district of Kerala, India. He obtained Alimiyya degree from Ilahiya College Tirurkad. He also completed a Master's degree in Arabic language and literature from Calicut University and a Masters degree in library and information science from Annamalai University in Tamil Nadu.

He was inclined towards writing since his school days and published articles in dailies in Kerala. He taught Arabic and Islamic studies at Perumpilavu Ansar English School for about five years. Then he took up the assignment as a teacher of Arabic and Islamic Studies at Ideal Indian School, Doha. Based on his outstanding performance and qualifications he was promoted as the head of department of the Arabic and Islamic Studies of the school. He continued in the post till he resigned in early 2006. He was also promoted as the Public Relations Officer of the school considering his potentials as a team leader.

In Doha he has been a regular writer and columnist in Arabic and English dailies. He was awarded Lokseva award by the Government of India for his work on Alcoholism in 1995. In 2005 he won the Anti Narcotic Award from the Kerala Government.

Among his published works are Spoken Arabic Made Easy, A Formula to Speak Arabic, Arabic Grammar Made Easy, A

Handbook on Arabic Grammar and Composition 'Improve Your Spoken Arabic', 'A Literary History of the Arabs', 'Catastrophies of Alcoholism', 'After S.S.L.C. What?', 'Technical Terms', 'Eid Mubarak,' 'Ramadan', Smoking or Health: Choice is Yours, Together for a Drug Free Society, Tobacco Free Sports, Play it Clean, Healthy Environment for Children, C.B.S.E. Arabic Series, and 'Love Revolution Through Blood Donation'.

PREFACE

Socio-cultural and educational importance of Arabic language has increased tremendously in the modern period for obvious reasons. As a result the care and concern in promoting this language as an international language of reputation has also become among the priority list of many educational institutions. Apart from its religious importance and dignity Arabic has been recognized as one of the most demanded languages in the world scenario and a number of educational institutions including schools, colleges and universities have come forward with various strategies and plans for imparting Arabic language.

In India, the Central Board of Secondary Education (C.B.S.E) has been offering Arabic as a second language in its All India Secondary School Examination curriculum (Class 10) and as an optional subject in its plus two course for a long time and the number of students offering it is on rise.

I had the privilege to introduce Arabic as a second language in Doha. I feel it has benefited hundreds of students and helped them score high marks in the public examination without much difficulty. It has also facilitated a good number of non-Indian students to pursue their education in Indian Schools.

It was in 1995 that I submitted my proposal for introducing Arabic as second and third language in the school and the management of Ideal Indian School Doha gave me the green signal to execute my proposal with immediate effect. The circular was sent to parents and the response was overwhelming. Every year the demand for Arabic is on rise and more and more students have come forward to opt Arabic as second or third language. All the students who offered Arabic fared very well in the public examinations and this made the other major Indian schools in the country to offer Arabic as a second language.

In my experience Arabic is the only subject in the C.B.S.E. stream , where all children passed with first class without undergoing any private tuitions. This speaks volumes about the advantages of opting Arabic as a second language and I feel many parents have realized this advantage.

Now Arabic has become one of the most demanded second languages in the Gulf region for many reasons. Firstly it is due to the employment market and wide range of openings to those who are bilinguals. Secondly children find it easy to learn and score maximum marks in the board examination.

Though the portions prescribed by C.B.S.E are simple, students often find it difficult to prepare for the examination in the absence of proper books catering to their demands and suitable to their standards. Several times my students asked me to suggest any book as a reference material and I was unable to guide them to any bilingual book. The only relevant material I found suitable was Al Nahwul Wadih which the students could not appreciate as the whole descriptions were in Arabic. This forced me to compile my notes and prepare a book as per the syllabus prescribed by the C.B.S.E. This is my humble attempt to present all topics suggested by the C.B.S.E. in its class 9 and 10 curriculum. I have tried my level best to make it as simple as possible by giving easy to remember examples that I feel any average student will be able to digest and reproduce without much difficulty. Repetition of examples is another salient feature of this book. It is a purposeful attempt I have made considering the level of students in the language.

Once the concepts are clear and you have at least two three examples to support it will serve the purpose even if you do not want to go to the depth of Arabic grammar. However understanding the grammatical concepts in its proper way and

10

practising them in our language applications would be the right way to enhance your language skills and ability.

This book mainly targets students who are offering Arabic as their second language in the C.B.S.E. stream though it can be used as a reference source for students of various levels. C.B.S.E gives much importance to the translation part and I have attempted to compile some five hundred Arabic sentences with English translation. Most of these sentences were taken from the previous question papers of C.B.S.E and some were taken from other language learning books. I am sure that if a child goes through these sentences and understands the format he can attempt translation of any simple sentence from Arabic to English and vice versa.

Composition part carries 10 marks in the C.B.S.E. examination. I have given model compositions on certain frequently asked topics and feel this will definitely help students in preparing their own short essays and compositions in the board examinations.

C.B.S.E has also introduced letter writing in its syllabus though it was never asked in the previous public examinations. However I have given some models of formal and informal letters as a guideline to the students. If children are thorough with these letters they will be able to attempt any question in this respect. Sample questions given as the last part of the book will guide students further on how to prepare for the board examination. The pattern asked every year being the same, the question papers of previous years can be of great use to all pupils in their preparations. It is highly recommended that students should solve these question papers and submit the answer scripts to their teachers for correction so that they will come to know where they are and what are the corrections to be made for scoring more marks in the examinations.

While bringing out this book I have to record my heartfelt thanks and gratitude to all friends and well-wishers for their encouragement and support.

I am really indebted to my former principals at the Ideal Indian School Dr.T. K. Muhammed and Mr. Ainsley Edgar for their creative support and motivation in my writings.

Special thanks are due to all well-wishers and patrons for their cooperation and support. I am thankful to my colleagues Regimon Augustine and to Mr. M. V. Joseph for their assistance in preparing this book.

With these words let me present this work before the students and general learners. My request is to point out errors and mistakes, if any and assure that suggestions and creative evaluations will be highly appreciated and looked in to while modifying the book.

Amanulla Vadakkangara
Doha

PART ONE

GRAMMAR

LESSON ONE

SENTENCE (الجملة المفيدة)

التَرْكِيبُ الذي يُفيدُ فَائِدَةً تَامَّةً يُسَمَّى جُمْلَةً مُفِيدَةً وَ يُسَمَّى أَيْضاً كَلَاماً. اَلْجُمْلَةُ الْمُفِيدَةُ قَدْ تَتَرَكَّبُ مِنْ كَلِمَتَيْنِ وَقَدْ تَتَرَكَّبُ مِنْ أَكْثَرَ. وَ كُلُّ كَلِمَةٍ فيهَا تُعَدُّ جُزْءٌ مِنْهاً.

A sentence is a group of words which gives a complete sense. In Arabic a sentence can be made up of two or more words and each of those word is considered to be a part of the sentence.

Examples

The garden is beautiful.	اَلْبُسْتَانُ جَمِيلٌ.	١)
The lesson is easy.	اَلدَّرْسُ سَهْلٌ.	٢)
The student is industrious.	اَلطَّالِبُ مُجْتَهِدٌ.	٣)
The school is big.	اَلْمَدْرَسَةُ كَبِيرَةٌ.	٤)
The car is new.	اَلسَّيَّارَةُ جَدِيدَةٌ.	٥)
The watch is old.	اَلسَّاعَةُ قَدِيمَةٌ.	٦)

Explanation

Observe the examples given and see the meaning expressed, we find that all examples consist of two words and convey a complete sense. If we remove any word from the sentence then the meaning will be incomplete. So it is to be understood that in order to convey a complete sense, minimum of two words are essential. We can have more than two words also. See the following examples.

The boy wrote the lesson.

١) كَتَبَ الْوَلَدُ الدَّرْسَ.

The girl sat on the chair.

٢) جَلَسَتِ الْبِنْتُ عَلَى الْكُرْسِيِّ.

The mother is cooking food.

٣) تَطْبُخُ الأُمُّ الطَّعَامَ.

Exercises

I. Fill in the blanks with appropriate words to form sentences.

(٦) الْمُدَرِّسُ الطَّوِيلُ ....   (١) اَلْعُصْفُورُ .... اَلْقَفَصِ

(٧) الْمُدِيرَةُ الْجَدِيدَةُ ....   (٢) اَلْوَلَدُ .... اَلْفَاكِهَةَ

(٨) الْبَيْتُ ....   (٣) اَلْبِنْتُ .... اَلثَّوْبَ

(٩) الطَّالِبُ ....   (٤) اَلْوَلَدُ الْمُجْتَهِدُ ....

(١٠) اَلْمُعَلِّمُ ....   (٥) اَلْمَسْجِدُ الْجَدِيدُ ....

II. Use the following words in sentence consisting of two words.

الْحَدِيْقَةُ — الشَّجَرَةُ — الأَزْهَارُ — الشَّمْسُ

III. Use the following words in sentence consisting of more than two words.

اَلْمَاءُ — اَلْفَاكِهَةُ — يَلْعَبُ — يَرْكَبُ

Answers

(٦) الْمُدَرِّسُ الطَّوِيلُ عَالِمٌ.   (١) اَلْعُصْفُورُ فِي الْقَفَصِ.

(٧) الْمُدِيرَةُ الْجَدِيدَةُ جَمِيلَةٌ.   (٢) اَلْوَلَدُ يَقْطَعُ الْفَاكِهَةَ.

15

(٣)   اَلْبِنْتُ تَغْسِلُ الثَّوْبَ.   (٨)   اَلْبَيْتُ نَظِيفٌ.

(٤)   اَلْوَلَدُ الْمُجْتَهِدُ نَاجِحٌ.   (٩)   الطَّالِبُ شَاطِرٌ.

(٥)   اَلْمَسْجِدُ الْجَدِيدُ قَرِيبٌ.   (١٠)   اَلْمُعَلِّمُ مُخْلِصٌ.

In Arabic the preferable pattern is VSO (Verb + Subject + Object).

| The park is clean. | (١) اَلْحَدِيقَةُ نَظِيفَةٌ. |

| The tree is big. | (٢) اَلشَّجَرَةُ كَبِيرَةٌ. |

| The flowers are fresh. | (٣) اَلْأَزْهَارُ طَازِجَةٌ. |

| The sun is rising. | (٤) اَلشَّمْسُ طَالِعَةٌ. |

| The boy drank water. | (١) شَرِبَ الْوَلَدُ الْمَاءَ. |

| The man eats fruit. | (٢) يَأْكُلُ الرَّجُلُ الْفَاكِهَةَ. |

| The student plays in the ground. | (٣) يَلْعَبُ الطَّالِبُ فِي الْمَلْعَبِ. |

| The passenger gets into the train. | (٤) يَرْكَبُ الْمُسَافِرُ الْقِطَارَ |

LESSON TWO

PARTS OF SPEECH (أقسام الكلمة)

اَلْكَلِمَةُ ثَلاَثَةُ أَنْوَاعٍ : اسْمٌ وَ فِعْلٌ وَ حَرْفٌ

اَلاسْمُ : كُلُّ لَفْظٍ يُسَمَّى بِهِ إِنْسَانٌ أَوْ حَيَوَانٌ أَوْ نَبَاتٌ أَوْ جَمَادٌ أَوْ أَيُّ شَيْئٍ آخَرَ.

اَلْفِعْلُ : كُلُّ لَفْظٍ يَدُلُّ عَلَى حُصُولِ عَمَلٍ فِيْ زَمَنٍ.

الْحَرْفُ: كُلُّ لَفْظٍ لاَ يَظْهَرُ مَعْنَاهُ كَامِلاً إِلاَّ مَعَ غَيْرِهِ.

Parts of speech are three: Noun, Verb, and Particle

NOUN: Name of a person, animal, plant, lifeless thing or anything else.

VERB: Any word referring to the occurrence of an action in a specific period of a time.

PARTICLE: Any word which does not express the meaning completely without being added to any other word.

Examples

Noun:

Khalid went to the market.   ١) ذَهَبَ خَالِدٌ إِلَى السُّوقِ.

Mohammed is a student.   ٢) مُحَمَّدٌ طَالِبٌ.

This is a horse.   ٣) هَذَا حِصَانٌ.

In these examples, the underlined words are Nouns.

Verb :

The boy wrote a story.	١) كَتَبَ الْوَلَدُ قِصَّةً.
Khalid teaches his son.	٢) يُعَلِّمُ خَالِدٌ ابْنَهُ.
Help the poor.	٣) اُنْصُرْ الْفَقِيرَ.

In these examples, the underlined words are Verbs.

Particle :

I went out of house in the morning.	١) خَرَجْتُ مِنَ الْبَيْتِ صَبَاحًا.
I returned from the school in the evening.	٢) رَجَعْتُ مِنَ الْمَدْرَسَةِ مَسَاءً.
I am going to the Mosque.	٣) أَذْهَبُ إِلَى الْمَسْجِدِ.

In these examples, the underlined words are prticles.

Exercises

1. Write three sentences consisting of two nouns each?
2. Write three sentences consisting of a noun and a verb?
3. Write three sentences with a noun, a verb, and a particle?
4. Fill in the blanks with suitable particles?

(١) يَسْبَحُ الْغُلَامُ .... النَّهْرِ   (٥) نَامَ الطِّفْلُ .... السَّرِيرِ

(٢) يَذْهَبُ التِّلْمِيذُ .... الْمَدْرَسَةِ   (٦) يَكْتُبُ الْمُدَرِّسُ .... السَّبُّورَةِ

(٣) قَطَعْتُ الْحَبْلَ .... السِّكِّينِ   (٧) سَأَلَ الطَّبِيبُ .... الْمَرَضِ

(٤) يَعُودُ الْغَرِيبُ .... بَلَدِهِ   (٨) هَذَا الْكِتَابُ .... مُحَمَّدٍ

Answers

I.

١) اَلْوَلَدُ مُجْتَهِدٌ.

٢) اَلْمَدْرَسَةُ كَبِيرَةٌ.

٣) اَلْبِنْتُ شَاطِرَةٌ.

II.

١) لَعِبَ الْوَلَدُ.

٢) كَتَبَ الطَّالِبُ.

٣) طَارَ الْغُرَابُ.

III.

١) لَعِبَ الْوَلَدُ فِي الْمَلْعَبِ.

٢) جَلَسَ الطَّالِبُ عَلَى الْكُرْسِيِّ.

٣) ذَهَبَ الْوَالِدُ إِلَى السُّوقِ.

IV.

(٥) نَامَ الطِّفْلُ عَلَى السَّرِيرِ.   (١) يَسْبَحُ الْغُلَامُ فِي النَّهْرِ.

(٦) يَكْتُبُ الْمُدَرِّسُ عَلَى السَّبُّورَةِ.   (٢) يَذْهَبُ التِّلْمِيذُ إِلَى الْمَدْرَسَةِ.

(٧) سَأَلَ الطَّبِيبُ عَنِ الْمَرَضِ.   (٣) قَطَعْتُ الْحَبْلَ بِالسِّكِّينِ.

(٨) هَذَا الْكِتَابُ لِمُحَمَّدٍ.   (٤) يَعُودُ الْغَرِيبُ إِلَى بَلَدِهِ.

LESSON THREE

NOMINAL SENTENCE (اَلْجُمْلَةُ الْاِسْمِيَّةُ)

كُلُّ جُمْلَةٍ تَتَرَكَّبُ مِنْ مُبْتَدَإٍ وَخَبَرٍ تُسَمَّى جُمْلَةً إِسْمِيَّةً.

A sentence consisting of a subject and a predicate is called a nominal sentence.

Examples :

The garden is beautiful.	١) اَلْبُسْتَانُ جَمِيلٌ.
The examination is easy.	٢) اَلْاِمْتِحَانُ سَهْلٌ.
The book is useful.	٣) اَلْكِتَابُ نَافِعٌ.

The Subject (اَلْمُبْتَدَأُ)

اَلْمُبْتَدَأُ اسْمٌ مَرْفُوْعٌ فِي أَوَّلِ الْجُمْلَةِ.

Subject is a noun in the nominative case which comes in the beginning of a sentence.

The Predicate (اَلْخَبَرُ)

اَلْخَبَرُ اسْمٌ مَرْفُوْعٌ يَكُوْنُ مَعَ الْمُبْتَدَإِ جُمْلَةً مُفِيْدَةً

Predicate is a noun in the nominative case which along with the subject gives a complete sense to the sentence.

Now by analyzing the examples based on these definitions we can see the words اَلْكِتَابُ — اَلْإِمْتِحَانُ — اَلْبُسْتَانُ are the subjects and نَافِعٌ — سَهْلٌ — جَمِيْلٌ are predicates.

Some more examples are given below:

The apple is sweet.	(١) اَلتُّفَّاحَةُ حُلْوَةٌ.
The photo is new.	(٢) اَلصُّورَةُ جَدِيدَةٌ.
Walking is useful.	(٣) اَلْمَشْيُ مُفِيدٌ.

In all these examples, If you say the first word alone the meaning will not be completed. The subject requires a predicate to express a complete sense.

Exercises.

1. Separate subjects and predicates from the following sentences.

(٦) اَلْفَقِيْرُ مَحْتَاجٌ.		(١) اَلدَّوَاةُ مَمْلُوْءَةٌ.	
(٧) اَلْحِذَاءُ جَدِيْدٌ.		(٢) اَلْمِزَاحُ مُضِرٌّ.	
(٨) اَلْحَدِيْقَةُ فَسِيْحَةٌ.		(٣) اَلْمُعَلِّمُ حَاضِرٌ.	
(٩) اَلشَّجَرَةُ مُثْمِرَةٌ.		(٤) اَلْهَوَاءُ نَقِيٌّ.	
(١٠) اَلْغَنِيُّ سَخِيٌّ.		(٥) اَلتَّاجِرُ أَمِيْنٌ.	

2. Fill in the blanks with suitable predicate.

(٦) اَلزَّهْرَةُ		(١) اَلثَّوْبُ	
(٧) اَلْقَرْيَةُ		(٢) اَلدَّرَّاجَةُ	
(٨) اَلْمَدِيْنَةُ		(٣) اَلسَّرِيْرُ	

21

(٤) اَلْكِتَابُ ....
(٩) اَلْبَحْرُ ....

(٥) اَلْغُرْفَةُ ....
(١٠) اَلْبَرْدُ ....

3. Fill in the blanks with suitable subjects.

(١) .... طَالِعَـــةٌ
(٦) .... بَاكِيَةٌ

(٢) .... صَغِيْرٌ
(٧) .... وَاسِعٌ

(٣) .... نَــائِمٌ
(٨) .... مُجْتَهِدٌ

(٤) .... مَذْبُوحَــةٌ
(٩) .... قَرِيْبٌ

(٥) .... عَلِيْلٌ
(١٠) .... جَمِيْلٌ

4. Define the structure of the following sentences.

(١) اَلسَّيَّارَةُ سَرِيْعَةٌ.

(٢) اَلْبِنْتُ جَمِيْلَةٌ.

(٣) اَلسَّمَاءُ مُمْطِرَةٌ.

(٤) اَلْجَوُّ مُعْتَدِلٌ.

(٥) اَلْبَرْدُ شَدِيْدٌ.

Answers

I

Subject		Predicate	
(١) اَلدَّوَاةُ		(١) مَمْلُوْءَةٌ	
(٢) اَلْمِزَاحُ		(٢) مُضِرٌّ	
(٣) اَلْمُعَلِّمُ		(٣) حَاضِرٌ	

(٤) اَلْهَوَاءُ   (٤) نَقِيٌّ

(٥) اَلتَّاجِرُ   (٥) أَمِينٌ

(٦) اَلْفَقِيرُ   (٦) مُحْتَاجٌ

(٧) اَلْحِذَاءُ   (٧) جَدِيدٌ

(٨) اَلْحَدِيقَةُ   (٨) فَسِيحَةٌ

(٩) اَلشَّجَرَةُ   (٩) مُثْمِرَةٌ

(١٠) اَلْغَنِيُّ   (١٠) سَخِيٌّ

II

(٦) اَلزَّهْرَةُ طَازَجَةٌ.   (١) اَلثَّوْبُ نَظِيفٌ.

(٧) اَلْقَرْيَةُ قَرِيبَةٌ.   (٢) اَلدَّرَّاجَةُ غَالِيَةٌ.

(٨) اَلْمَدِينَةُ بَعِيدَةٌ.   (٣) اَلسَّرِيرُ مَكْسُورٌ.

(٩) اَلْبَحْرُ شَدِيدٌ.   (٤) اَلْكِتَابُ مُفِيدٌ.

(١٠) اَلْبَرْدُ قَاسٍ.   (٥) اَلْغُرْفَةُ مَفْتُوحَةٌ.

III

(٦) اَلْبِنْتُ بَاكِيَةٌ.   (١) اَلشَّمْسُ طَالِعَةٌ.

(٧) اَلْمَلْعَبُ وَاسِعٌ.   (٢) اَلْوَلَدُ صَغِيرٌ.

(٨) اَلطَّالِبُ مُجْتَهِدٌ.   (٣) اَلطِّفْلُ نَائِمٌ.

(٩) اَلامْتِحَانُ قَرِيبٌ.   (٤) اَلْبَقَرَةُ مَذْبُوحَةٌ.

(١٠) اَلْبُسْتَانُ جَمِيلٌ.   (٥) اَلْعَامِلُ عَلِيلٌ.

IV

١) اَلسَّيَّارَةُ سَرِيعَةٌ: اَلسَّيَّارَةُ — مُبْتَدَأٌ مَرْفُوعٌ بِالضَّمَّةِ،

سَرِيعَةٌ — خَبَرٌ مَرْفُوعٌ بِالضَّمَّةِ

٢) اَلْبِنْتُ جَمِيلَةٌ: اَلْبِنْتُ — مُبْتَدَأٌ مَرْفُوعٌ بِالضَّمَّةِ،

جَمِيلَةٌ — خَبَرٌ مَرْفُوعٌ بِالضَّمَّةِ

٣) اَلسَّمَاءُ مُمْطِرَةٌ: اَلسَّمَاءُ — مُبْتَدَأٌ مَرْفُوعٌ بِالضَّمَّةِ،

مُمْطِرَةٌ — خَبَرٌ مَرْفُوعٌ بِالضَّمَّةِ

٤) اَلْجَوُّ مُعْتَدِلٌ: اَلْجَوُّ — مُبْتَدَأٌ مَرْفُوعٌ بِالضَّمَّةِ،

مُعْتَدِلٌ — خَبَرٌ مَرْفُوعٌ بِالضَّمَّةِ

٥) اَلْبَرْدُ شَدِيدٌ: اَلْبَرْدُ — مُبْتَدَأٌ مَرْفُوعٌ بِالضَّمَّةِ،

شَدِيدٌ — خَبَرٌ مَرْفُوعٌ بِالضَّمَّةِ

LESSON FOUR

KANA AND HER SISTERS (كَانَ وَ أَخَوَاتُهَا)

تَدْخُلُ كَانَ عَلَى الْمُبْتَدَإِ وَالْخَبَرِ فَتَرْفَعُ الأَوَّلَ وَيُسَمَّى اسْمَهَا وَتَنْصِبُ الثَّانِيَ وَيُسَمَّى خَبَرَهَا. مِثْلَ كَانَ فِيمَا تَقَدَّمَ صَارَ وَلَيْسَ وَأَصْبَحَ وَأَمْسَى وَأَضْحَى وَظَلَّ وَبَاتَ وَتُسَمَّى هَذِهِ الأَفْعَالُ أَخَوَاتَ كَانَ. لِكُلِّ فِعْلٍ مِنْ هَذِهِ الأَفْعَالِ مُضَارِعٌ وَأَمْرٌ يَعْمَلاَنِ عَمَلِ الْمَاضِي الاَّ لَيْسَ فَلاَ يَأْتِي مِنْهَا مُضَارِعٌ وَلاَ أَمْرٌ.

Kana and her sisters enter the nominal sentences. When it comes the subject will be in the nominative case and it is called its noun and the predicate will be in accusative case and it is called its predicate. The present and imperative tense of these verbs except *Laysa* also do the same action. For Laysa there won't be present and imperative forms.

Examples:

The boy is industrious.	اَلْوَلَدُ مُجْتَهِدٌ.	(١
The boy was industrious.	كَانَ الْوَلَدُ مُجْتَهِدًا.	
The dress is short.	اَلثَّوْبُ قَصِيرٌ.	(٢
The dress became short.	صَارَ الثَّوْبُ قَصِيرًا.	

٣)   اَلْخَادِمُ قَوِيٌّ.   The servant is strong.

كَانَ الْخَادِمُ قَوِيًّا.   The servant was strong.

٤)   اَلْجَوُّ مَمْطِرٌ.   The weather is rainy.

أَصْبَحَ الْجَوُّ مَمْطِرًا.   The weather became rainy.

٥)   اَلْعَامِلُ مُتْعَبٌ.   The worker is tired.

أَمْسَى الْعَامِلُ مُتْعَبًا.   The worker became tired (In the evening).

٦)   اَلشَّارِعُ مُزْدَحِمٌ.   The road is busy.

أَضْحَى الشَّارِعُ مُزْدَحِمًا.   The road became busy.

٧)   اَلْغُبَارُ ثَائِرٌ.   The dust is flying.

ظَلَّ الْغُبَارُ ثَائِرًا.   The dust became flying.

٨)   اَلْمَرِيضُ بَاكٍ.   The patient is crying.

بَاتَ الْمَرِيضُ بَاكِيًا.   The patient stayed in the night crying.

Exercise :

1. Identify noun and predicate of "Kana and her Sisters" in the following sentences

(٥)   لَيْسَ الْمَيْدَانُ فَسِيحًا.   (١)   كَانَ مُحَمَّدٌ شُجَاعًا.

(٦)   أَمْسَى الْغَنِيُّ فَقِيرًا.   (٢)   أَصْبَحَ الْحِصَانُ جَائِعًا.

(٧)   أَضْحَى السَّجِينُ طَلِيقًا.   (٣)   صَارَ الْأَوَّلُ آخِرًا.

(٨)   ظَلَّ الْعِنَبُ كَثِيرًا.   (٤)   بَاتَ الْكَلْبُ نَائِمًا.

2. Add 'Kana' or 'Sara' or 'Lysa' or 'Adha' in the following sentences:

(٤)   اَلتِّلْمِيْذُ نَشِيْطٌ.   (١)   اَلْبَابُ مَفْتُوْحٌ.

(٢)‏ اَلْجَوُّ حَارٌّ.‏ (٥)‏ اَلْخَادِمُ نَائِمٌ.‏

(٣)‏ اَلْوَلَدُ مَرِيضٌ.‏

Answers :

I

خَبَـــرٌ	اِسْـــمٌ
شُجَاعًا	مَحْمُوْدٌ
جَائِعًا	حِصَانٌ
آخِرًا	اَلْأَوَّلُ
نَائِمًا	اَلْكَلْبُ
فَسِيْحًا	مَيْدَانٌ
فَقِيْرًا	اَلْغَنِيُّ
طَلِيْقًا	اَلسَّجِيْنُ
كَثِيْرًا	اَلْعِنَبُ

II

٤)‏ أَصْبَحَ التِّلْمِيْذُ نَشِيْطًا.‏ ١)‏ كَانَ الْبَابُ مَفْتُوْحًا.‏

٥)‏ لَيْسَ الْخَادِمُ نَائِمًا.‏ ٢)‏ صَارَ الْجَوُّ حَارًّا.‏

٣)‏ لَيْسَ الْوَلَدُ مَرِيْضًا.‏

LESSON FIVE

INNA AND HER SISTERS (إِنَّ وَ أَخَوَاتُهَا)

إِنَّ وَ أَنَّ وَ كَأَنَّ وَ لَكِنَّ وَ لَيْتَ وَ لَعَلَّ تَدْخُلُ عَلَى الْمُبْتَدَإِ وَالْخَبَرِ فَتَنْصُبُ الْمُبْتَدَأَ وَ تُسَمَّى إِسْمَهَا وَتَرْفَعُ الْخَبَرَ وَتُسَمَّى خَبَرَهَا.

Inna and her Sisters enter the nominal sentence then the subject will be in accusative and the predicate will be in the nominative case.

Examples :

Allah is the most forgiving.	اَللهُ غَفُوْرٌ .	(١)
Surely Allah is the most forgiving.	إِنَّ اَللهَ غَفُوْرٌ.	
The examination is near.	اَلْاِمْتِحَانُ قَرِيْبٌ .	(٢)
I knew that the examination is near.	عَلِمْتُ أَنَّ اَلْإِمْتِحَانَ قَرِيْبٌ.	
The book is a teacher.	اَلْكِتَابُ أُسْتَاذٌ.	(٣)
The book is like a teacher.	كَأَنَّ الْكِتَابَ أُسْتَاذٌ.	
The furniture is old.	اَلْأَثَاثُ قَدِيْمٌ.	(٤)
The house is new but the furniture is old.	اَلْبَيْتُ جَدِيْدٌ وَلَكِنَّ الْأَثَاثَ قَدِيمٌ.	
The fruit is ripe.	اَلْفَاكِهَةُ نَاضِجَةٌ.	(٥)

I wish the fruit is ripe.	لَيْتَ الْفَاكِهَةَ نَاضِجَةٌ.
The patient is sleeping.	(٦) اَلْمَرِيْضُ نَائِمٌ.
Perhaps the patient is sleeping.	لَعَلَّ اَلْمَرِيْضَ نَائِمٌ.

Exercises :

1. Identify the noun and the predicate of 'Inna and her sisters' from the following sentences.

٤) ليت التلميذ مجتهد.		١) لعل التفاح كبير.	
٥) إن النظافة واجبة.		٢) لعل التاجر رابح.	
٦) امتنع المطر لكن السحاب كثير.		٣) وجدت ان العقربة متينة.	

II. Add 'Inna' or 'Lytha' or 'Laalla' in the following.

٤) البائع أمين.		١) الشارع واسع.	
٥) الماء كرر.		٢) النجوم لامعة.	
٦) الخبر صحيح.		٣) المسافر قادم.	

Answers:

I.

اسم — خبر		اسم — خبر	
٤) التلميذ ــ مجتهد		١) التفاح ــ كبير	
٥) النظافة ــ واجبة		٢) التاجر ــ رابح	
٦) السحاب ــ كثير		٣) العقربة ــ متينة	

II

١)   ليت الشارع واسع   ٤)   ليت البائع أمين

٢)   إنّ النجوم لامعة   ٥)   إنّ الماء كرر

٣)   لعل المسافر قادم   ٦)   لعل الخبر صحيح

LESSON SIX

VERBAL SENTENCE (اَلْجُمْلَةُ الْفِعْلِيَّةُ)

> كُلُّ جُمْلَةٍ تَتَرَكَّبُ مِنْ فِعْلٍ وَ فَاعِلٍ تُسَمَّى جُمْلَةً فِعْلِيَّةً

> A sentence consisting of a verb and doer is called a Verbal sentence

Verbs are divided into transitive and intransitive verbs. In transitive verbs the doer will be accompanied by an object also.

Examples.

The child slept.	١) نَامَ الطِّفْلُ.
The craw flew.	٢) طَارَ الْغُرَابُ.
The man laughed.	٣) ضَحِكَ الرَّجُلُ.

If we analyze these sentences we can see all of them have started with verbs what is the other word came along with the verbs. It is the subject. So we can say that all sentences starting with a verb are consisting of a verb and a subject is called a **verbal sentence.**

In the example given these were verbs and doer only. But as I pointed out in the beginning these can be object also. See the following sentences.

١) كَتَبَ الْوَلَدُ الدَّرْسَ

٢) تَطْبَخُ الأُمُّ الطَّعَامَ

٣) يَقْرَأُ الأَبُ الْجَرِيْدَةَ

In these examples — اَلدَّرْسَ — اَلطَّعَامَ — اَلْجَرِيْدَةَ are objects

VERBS (اَلْفِعْلُ)

Verbs can be classified as past , present/future commanding and probability

Past Tense (اَلْفِعْلُ اَلْمَاضِيُّ)

> كُلُّ لَفْظٍ يَدُلُّ عَلَى حُصُوْلِ شَيْئٍ فِي زَمَنٍ مَاضٍ

Any word referring to the occurrence of an action in the past

Examples : كَتَبَ ــ جَلَسَ ــ نَجَحَ

If you put مَا before a past tense then you will get the negative meaning

Examples:

The boy wrote – The boy did not write	كَتَبَ الوَلَدُ ــ مَا كَتَبَ الوَلَدُ	١)
The girl sat – The girl did not sit	جَلَسَتْ البِنتُ ــ مَا جَلَسَتْ البِنتُ	٢)
The child slept – The child did not sleep	نَامَ الطِّفْلُ ــ مَا نَامَ الطِّفْلُ	٣)

Past tense verbs can be divided as triliteral and quadriliteral verbs. A past tense must have minimum three letters and it can have maximum six letters. But original letter will be three or four.

See some examples :

The servant opened the room	١)	فَتَحَ الخَادِمُ الغُرْفَةَ
The manager honoured the sincere worker	٢)	أَكْرَمَ المُدِيرُ العَامِلَ المُخْلِصَ
The earth shivered in Asia	٣)	زُلْزَلَتِ الأَرْضُ في آسِيَا

Past tense can be analyzed as:

Positive	مثبت	Negative	منفي
Triliteral	ثلاثي	Quadriliteral	رباعي
Subject Known	معروف	Subject Unknown	مجهول

LESSON EIGHT

PRESENT TENSE (الفعل المضارع)

Once we have past tense within. It is very easy to make it into present. Just follow these steps.

1. Bring any of the letter of present tense in the beginning of the past tense (حروف المضارعة). Letters of the present tense are (أ ، ت ، ي ، ن). They are brought based on the subject. For example, when I come as the subject we have to bring (أ). Where and when we come as subject (ن) is brought. (ت) is brought when the subject is you or she and (ي) is brought when the subject is he / she. To set a clear picture about this you should learn the conjugation of present tense (تصريف الفعل المضارع)

2. Remove the sound of the first basic letter

3. Give (ضمة) to the last letter

See how the verbs are changed into present tense:

نَصَرَ ــ يَنْصُرُ ــ تَنْصُرُ ــ أَنْصُرُ ــ نَنْصُرُ

نَظَرَ ــ يَنْظُرُ ــ أَنْظُرُ ــ نَنْظُرُ ــ تَنْظُرُ

جَلَسَ ــ يَجْلِسُ ــ أَجْلِسُ ــ نَجْلِسُ ــ تَجْلِسُ

If we add (لا) before a present tense we will get negative meaning

Examples :

1) يَكْتُبُ الوَلَدُ ــ لا يَكْتُبُ الوَلَدُ

The boy writes – The boy does not write

2) تَجْلِسُ البِنْتُ ــ لا تَجْلِسُ البِنْتُ

The girl sits – The girl does not sit

3) يَنْظُرُ الرَّجُلُ ــ لا يَنْظُرُ الرَّجُلُ

The man looks – The man does not look

In Arabic present and future tense are one and the same. To differentiate present and future (س) and (سوف) are added before the present tense. س is used for near future and سوف is used for distant future.

Near Future

Examples:

سأذهب إلى السوق بعد غد

I will go to the market day after tomorrow.

سيجيئ أخي مساء اليوم

My brother will come today evening.

سيخرج القطار بعد ساعة

The train will go after one hour.

Distant Future

Examples:

سوف أذهب إلى السعودية العربية

I will go Saudi Arabia

سوف أكون مديرا

I will be a Manager

سوف يكون الجو باردا

The weather will be cold

Present tense - Nominal case (رفع الفعل المضارع)

يرفع الفعل المضارع إذا لم تسبقه أداة من أدوات النواصب او الجوازم.

Present tense will be in nominal case if not preceded by letters of accusation and jussive cases

Examples :

The boy writes the lesson	١) يَكْتُبُ الوَلَدُ الدَّرْسَ
The child drinks milk	٢) يَشْرَبُ الطِّفْلُ الحَلِيبَ
The servant cleans the house	٣) يُنَظِّفُ الْخَادِمُ البَيْتَ

We can make a variation form from a given present tense. This process is called conjugation (تصريف) in grammar. How this is done is explained in the following example:

يَكْتُبُونَ	يَكْتُبَانِ	يَكْتُبُ
يَكْتُبْنَ	تَكْتُبَانِ	تَكْتُبُ
تَكْتُبُونَ	تَكْتُبَانِ	تَكْتُبُ
تَكْتُبْنَ	تَكْتُبَانِ	تَكْتُبِينَ
	نَكْتُبُ	أَكْتُبُ

Once you are through with one verb you can make variation form from any verbs.

(Note: أ, و and ي are known as week letters. If any of these letters come in the beginning, middle or at the end there can be some changes)

Present Tense – Accusative case (نصب الفعل المضارع)

ينصب الفعل المضارع إذا سبقه أحد النواصب الأربعة وهي:

أن ــ لن ــ إذن ــ كي

Present tense will be in accusative case if it is preceded by أَنْ — لَنْ — إِذَنْ — كَيْ

Examples:

I want to learn Arabic language	١) أُرِيدُ اَنْ اَدْرُسَ اللُّغَةَ العَرَبِيَّةَ
The lazy will never succeed	٢) لَنْ يَنْجَحَ الكَسْلاَنُ
I will visit Doha, then you will stay with us	٣) سَأَزُورُ الدَّوْحَةَ اِذَنْ تُقِيمَ عِنْدَنَا
I came to study	٤) جِئْتُ لِكَيْ اَتَعَلَّمَ

Present Tense – Jussive case (جزم الفعل المضارع)

يجزم الفعل المضارع إذا سبقه حرف جازم كالحروف التالية وهي: لم ولا الناهية وإن

Present Tense will be in Jussive case if it is preceded by لَمْ، لا الناهية، إن

Examples:

The boy did not attend the class	١) لَمْ يَحْضُرْ الوَلَدُ الدَّرْسَ
Don't play in the class	٢) لا تَلْعَبْ فِي الفَصْلِ
If you work hard, you will succeed	٣) إِنْ تَجْتَهِدْ تَنْجَحْ

LESSON NINE

FORMATION OF IMPERATIVE (فعل الأمر)

> فعل الأمر هو كل فعل يطلب به حصول شيئ في زمن المستقبل

> The imperative verb is one that demands the occurrence of an action in the future.

Imperative verbs are formed from the present tense. To make imperative verb from the third person we need to bring لِ before the verb jussive case at the end

Example :

يكتب ــ ليكتب ، يجلس ــ ليجلس ، يذهب ــ ليذهب

Six forms of imperative third person will be like this

ليذهب ــ ليذهبا ــ ليذهبوا

لتذهب ــ لتذهبا ــ ليذهبن

There are various ways to make imperative form from the second person, I am explaining here the most common ways.

1. Bring the present tense

2. Delete the letters of present tense (حرف المضارعة)

3. In triliteral verbs if the letter after it is without any vowels (with sukoon) then bring *Hamzathul wasl.*

4. If the second last letter is with *Fathah* or *Kasrah*, give *Kesrah* to the Hamza and if the second last letter is *Dammah* (ضمة) give *Dhammah* to *Hamza*

5. If the verb has more than three letters your will have to give *Fathah* or *Kasrah* to Hamza

6. Give Jussive case at the end

7. If the letter after deleting the letter of present tense is with vowels then give jussive case at the end only.

Examples:

1. كَتَبَ ــ يَكْتُبُ ــ تَكْتُبُ ــ تَكْتُبُ ــ أُكْتُبْ

(*Hamza* with *Dhammah* because the second last letter has *Dammah*)

2. جَلَسَ ــ يَجْلِسُ ــ تَجْلِسُ ــ تَجْلِسُ ــ إجْلِس

(*Hamza* with *Kasrah* because the second last letter has *Kasrah*)

3. فَتَحَ ــ يَفْتَحُ ــ تَفْتَحُ ــ تَفْتَحُ ــ إِفْتَحْ

(*Hamza* with *Kasrah* because the second last letter has *Fathah*)

4. أَسْلَمَ ــ يُسْلِمُ ــ تُسْلِمُ ــ تُسْلِمُ ــ أَسْلِمْ

(*Hamza* has *fathah* because the verb has four letters)

5. وَقَفَ ــ يَقِفُ ــ تَقِفُ ــ تَقِفُ ــ قِفْ

(Nothing is added as the letter after the letter of present tense is with vowels)

How to make various forms from the imperative verbs is shown below:

1. أُكْتُبْ ــ أُكْتُبَا ــ أُكْتُبُوا ــ أُكْتُبِي ــ أُكْتُبَا ــ أُكْتُبْنَ

2. أِجْلِسْ ــ إِجْلِسَا ــ إِجْلِسُوا ــ إِجْلِسِي ــ إِجْلِسَا ــ إِجْلِسْنَ

3. أَسْلِمْ ــ أَسْلِمَا ــ أَسْلِمُوا ــ أَسْلِمِيْ ــ أَسْلِمَا ــ أَسْلَمْنَ

4. قِفْ ــ قِفَا ــ قِفُوا ــ قِفِي ــ قِفَا ــ قِفْنَ

Usually the imperative form is made from the first person as it will give a meaningful message

LESSON TEN

PROHIBITIVE COMMAND (فعل النهي)

> Prohibitive command is the verb which prohibits an action in future, so it is also made from the present tense. To make prohibitive command we need to bring لا before the present tense and give jussive case at the end.

Examples:

يَذْهَبُ (He goes), لاَ يَذْهَبْ (He should not go), تَذْهَبُ (You go), لاَ تَذْهَبْ (You should not go)

How the prohibitive command is made is shown below:

لاَ يَذْهَبُوا — لاَ يَذْهَبَا — لاَ يَذْهَبْ

لاَ يَذْهَبْنَ — لاَ تَذْهَبَا — لاَ تَذْهَبْ

لاَ تَذْهَبُوا — لاَ تَذْهَبَا — لا تَذْهَبْ

لاَ تَذْهَبْنَ — لاَ تَذْهَبَا — لاَ تَذْهَبِي

لاَ نَذْهَبْ — لا أَذْهَبْ

Even though we can make prohibitive command from all forms generally the form of second persons are widely used

١. لا تَكْتُبُوا — لا تَكْتُبَا — لا تَكْتُبْ

لا تَكْتُبْنَ — لا تَكْتُبَا — لا تَكْتُبِي

٢. لا تَفْتَحْ — لا تَفْتَحَا — لا تَفْتَحُوا

لا تَفْتَحِي — لا تَفْتَحَا — لا تَفْتَحْنَ

٣. لا تَجْلِسْ — لا تَجْلِسَا — لا تَجْلِسُوا

لا تَجْلِسِي — لا تَجْلِسَا — لا تَجْلِسْنَ

LESSON ELEVEN

THE DOER (الفاعل)

الفاعل اسم مرفوع تقدمه فعل ودل على الذي فعل الفعل

The doer is a noun in the nominative case preceeded by a verb and refers that it does / has done the action.

Examples:

١) كَتَبَ الوَلَدُ الدَّرْسَ	The boy wrote the lesson
٢) شَرِبَ الطِّفْلُ الحَلِيبَ	The child drank milk
٣) يَقْرَأُ الْمُعَلِّمُ الْجَرِيدَةَ	The teacher reads the newspaper

Explanation:

Observe the given examples. The underlined words الوَلد / الطفل / المعلم in these sentences are nouns in the nominative case. These words are preceded by verbs and they express that these do or have done the action. That is why they are called the doers in these sentences.

Exercises :

I. Find out the doer from the following sentences:

١) صَاحَ الدِّيكُ   ٢) جَاءَ الطَّبِيبُ

(٣) أشغل العامل   (٤) وَقَفَ الثَّورُ

(٥) لَعبَ الأوْلاَدُ   (٦) زَرَعَ الفَلاَّحُ

(٧) بَكَى الطِّفلُ   (٨) لَدَغَ الثَّعْبَانُ

(٩) حَضَرَ الغَائِبُ   (١٠) كَتَبَ الوَلَدُ

2. Form sentences by putting proper doers to the following verbs

(١) نبح   (٢) يضحك   (٣) يبكي

(٤) يشرب   (٥) سافر   (٦) يركب

(٧) عطش

3. Form sentences by putting proper verbs to the following nouns

(١) التلميذ   (٢) الثعلب   (٣) الرجل

(٤) السفينة   (٥) الخادم

Answers:

I.

(١) الديك   (٢) الطبيب   (٣) العامل

(٤) الثور   (٥) الأولاد   (٦) الفلاح

(٧) الطفل   (٨) الثعبان   (٩) الغائب

(١٠) الولد

II.

(١) نَبَحَ الكَلْبُ   (٢) يَضْحَكُ الوَلَدُ

(٣) يَبْكِي الطِّفْلُ   (٤) يَشْرَبُ خالد

45

(٥) سَافَرَ المُدِيرُ   (٦) يَرْكَبُ عَلَى القِطَارِ

(٧) عَطِشَ الرَّجُلُ

III.

(١) نَجَحَ التِّلْمِيذُ   (٢) خَطَفَ الثَّعْلَبُ الدِّيكَ

(٣) ذَهَبَ الرَّجُلُ   (٤) تَجْرِي السَّفِينَةُ فِي البَحْرِ

(٥) يُنَظِّفُ الخَادِمُ البَيْتَ

THE OBJECT (المفعول به)

الْمَفْعُولُ بِهِ اسم منصوب وقع عليه فعل الفاعل

Object is a noun in the accusative case on which the action of the doer takes place

Examples :

The boy wrote the lesson	١) كتب الولد الدرس
The mother cooks food	٢) يطبخ الأم الطعام
The man drinks tea	٣) يشرب الرجل الشاي

In these examples the last word refers first the action of the doer was done or being done they are called as object.

Exercises:

1. Find out the object from the following examples.

(١)   مَزَّقَ الفَلاَّحُ الوَرَقَ   (٢)   حَلَبَت الفَتَاةُ البَقَرَةَ

(٣)   أَيقَظَ الرَّعْدُ النَّائِمَ   (٤)   صَنَعَ النَّجَّارُ كُرْسِيًا

(٥)   رَمَى الصَّيَّادُ الشَّبَكَةَ

2. Form sentences by making the following nouns as object.

(٣) النافذة   (٢) الموز   (١) الدرس

(٥) الماء   (٤) الطاولة

Answers:

I.

(١) الورق   (٢) البقرة   (٣) النائم

(٤) كرسيا   (٥) الشبكة

II.

(١) كَتَبَ الوَلَدُ الدَّرسَ   (٢) أَكَلَ محمد الْمَوْزَ   (٣) فَتَحَ الْخَادِمُ النَافِذَةَ

(٤) صَنَعَ النَّجَّارُ الطَّاوِلَةَ   (٥) شَرِبَ الطِفْلُ الْمَاءَ

LESSON THIRTEEN

ADJECTIVE AND THE NOUN QUALIFIED
(الصفة والموصوف (مركب وصفي) النعت والمنعوت)

النعت لفظ يدل على صفة في اسم قبله ويسمى الإسم الموصوف
منعوتا الصفة تتبع الموصوف في رفعه ونصبه وجره

Adjective (صفة) is a word which qualifies a noun. The noun which is being qualified is موصوف. Adjective will follow the noun qualified in nominative, accusative, and genitive case

Examples:

This is a new pen	هذَا قَلَمٌ جَدِيدٌ	١)
I bought a new pen	اشْتَرَيْتُ قَلَمًا جَدِيدًا	
I wrote with a new pen	كَتَبْتُ بِقَلَمٍ جَدِيدٍ	
This is an expensive car	هَذِه سَيَّارَةٌ غَالِيَةٌ	٢)
I saw an expensive car	رَأَيْتُ سَيَّارَةً غَالِيَةً	
I sat in an expensive car	جَلَسْتُ في سَيَّارَةٍ غَالِيَةٍ	
That is a big school	تلْكَ مَدْرَسَةٌ كَبِيرَةٌ	٣)
I saw a big school	رَأَيْتُ مَدْرَسَةً كَبِيرَةً	
I studied in a big school	دَرَسْتُ في مَدْرَسَةٍ كَبِيرَةٍ	

See some more examples:

١. الْوَلَدُ الْمُؤَدَّبُ مَحْبُوبٌ.

٢. الْبَيْتُ الْجَدِيدُ نَظِيفٌ.

٣. لا تَشْرَبْ الْمَاءَ الْكَرَرَ.

٤. الْمَسْجِدُ الْكَبِيرُ قَرِيبٌ.

٥. الْمُدَرِّسُ الْجَدِيدُ عَالِمٌ.

LESSON FOURTEEN

GENITIVE CASE TO THE NOUN
(جر الإسم (مركب جري))

يجر الاسم إذا سبقه حرف من حروف الجر الآتية وهي : من و إلى
وعن وعلى وفي والباء واللام

A noun will be in the genitive case (مجرور) if it is preceded
by من/ إلى / عن / على / في / ب / ل. These letter are called
letters of genitive case (حروف الجر)

Examples:

The teacher returned from the school	رَجَعَ الْمُدَرِّسُ مِنَ الْمَدرَسَة	١)
I am going to the market	أذهَبُ إلَى السُّوقِ	٢)
I kept the book in the table	وَضَعتُ الكِتَابَ عَلَى الطَّاوِلَة	٣)
The teacher asked about Khalid	سَأَلَ الْمُدَرِّسُ عَن خَالِدٍ	٤)
I kept the book in the bag	وَضَعتُ الكِتَابَ في الْحَقِيبَة	٥)
I wrote with pen	كَتَبتُ بِالقَلَمِ	٦)
The prize is for the winner	الْجَائِزَةُ لِلسَّابِقِ	٧)

Some more examples are given below:

(٨)	يَسْقُطُ النَّمِرُ عَلَى الأرضِ	(١)	نَزَلَ المَطَرُ مِنَ السَّمَاءِ
(٩)	ينبح الكَلْبُ في البُستَانِ	(٢)	يأتِي السَّمَكُ مِنَ البَحْرِ
(١٠)	دَخَلَ المُجرِمُ في السِّجْنِ	(٣)	سَعَى الجَيشُ إلَى المَيدَانِ
(١١)	قَشَرتُ الفَاكِهَةَ بالسِّكِّينِ	(٤)	سَارَت المَاشِيَةُ إلَى الحَقلِ
(١٢)	يَتَقَاتَلُ الجُنُودُ بالسُّيُوفِ	(٥)	يَنْزِلُ الجُنديُّ عَنِ الحصَانِ
(١٣)	الجَوابُ للسؤال	(٦)	يَذهَبُ الخَوْفُ عَنِ الطِّفْلِ
(١٤)	اشتريت قُفْلا للخَزَانَةِ	(٧)	يَطُوفُ الخَشَبُ عَلى النَّارِ

LESSON FIFTEEN

DEMONSTRATIVE PRONOUNS
(أسماء الإشارة)

أسماء الإشارة أسماء تدل على مشار إليه

Demonstrative pronouns are words referring to specific things pointed to it commonly used demonstrative pronouns are (ذا ، ذه ، ذان ، تان ، أولاء)

أسماء الإشارة هي:

Masculine singular	—	ذا ــ للمفرد المذكر
Feminine singular	—	ذه ــ للمفرد المؤنث
Masculine Dual	—	ذان ــ للمثنى المذكر
Feminine Dual	—	تان ــ للمثنى المؤنث
Plural of masculine and feminine (Human beings only)	—	أولاء ــ لجمع العقلاء من ذكور أو إناث ــ

اسم الإشارة للمثنى المذكر أو المؤنث يعامل معاكلة المثنى فيكون بالألف في حالة الرفع وبالياء في حالتي النصب والجر

Demonstrative pronouns for masculine and feminine dual will work as per the system of dual and it will be with 'Alif' in nominative and with 'Ya' in the accusative and genitive case

Examples :

١)	ذا رجل شريف	This is a gentle man
٢)	هذا كتاب نافع	This is a useful book
٣)	ذه إمرأة تعتني بأولادها	This is a lady who takes care of her children
٤)	هذه حجرة واسعة	This is a vast room
٥)	ذان ولدان مهذبان	These two are civilized boys
٦)	إن هذين فائزان	Surely, these two are winners
٧)	تان وردتان مفتحان	These two roses are open
٨)	إن هاتين بنتين مطيعتان	Surely, these two girls are obedient
٩)	أولاء تجار صادقون	They are trustful traders
١٠)	هؤلاء صناع ماهرون	These are expert producers
١١)	أولاء بنات نظيفات	Those are clean girls
١٢)	هؤلاء تلميذات لطيفات	These are soft students

LESSON SIXTEEN

THE GENITIVE OF POSSESSION
المضاف والمضاف اليه (مركب اضافي)

المضاف اسم نسب الى اسم بعده فتعرف بسبب هذه النسبة او تخصص.

المضاف يحذف تنوينه عند الاضافة اذا كان منونا قبلها وتحذف نونه اذا كان مثنى او جمع مذكر سالما

المضاف اليه اسم يأتي بعد المضاف وهو مجرور.

Mudaf is a noun added or joined to a noun following it. It becomes known or specific because of this joining.

Usually a noun is joined in this pattern to express possessive meaning. That is why this is termed in grammar as genitive of possession.

Mudaf will lose it's nunation while joining as it will lose its noon if it is Dual or Sound Masculine Plural.

Mudafun Ilayhi is the noun which comes after *Mudaf* and it is always in genitive case.

A noun followed by a genitive case can not take the definite article in any case, eg:

We played in the courtyard of the school.

١) لَعِبْنَا فِي فِنَاء الْمَدْرَسَة

Keep away from bad friends.	٢) ابْتَعِدْ عَن قَرِين السُّوء
I got into the morning train.	٣) رَكِبتُ قطَارَ الصَّبَاح
I washed both hands of the child	٤) غسلت يدي الطفل
Both tires of the bicycle were broken	٥) انكَسَرَتْ عَجَلَتَا الدَّرَّاجَة
I helped two children of the teacher.	٦) سَاعَدتُ ولدي المدَرِّس
Drivers of the cars hurried.	٧) أسرَعَ سائقُو السيارة
Teachers of the school came.	٨) جَاءَ مُعَلمُو المَدرَسَة
Muslims of India are active.	٩) مُسلمُو الهند شَاطِرُونَ

Observe the underlined words. In all these examples the first noun is added to the second noun for a specific purpose of expressing its possession. In such cases the noun added is called *Mudaf* and the noun to which it is added is called as *Mudafun Ilayhi*.

Mudafun Ilayhi will be always in genitive case.

FORMATION OF *ISM FAEL* AND *ISM MAFOOL*

اسم الفاعل واسم المفعول

اسم الفاعل:

اسم الفاعل : اسم الفاعل اسم مصوغ للدلالة على ما فعل الفعل. وهو من الثلاثي على صورة فاعل ومن غير الثلاثي على صورة مضارعه بابدال حرف المضارعة ميما مضمومة وكسر ما قبل الآخر

Ism Fael (اسم الفاعل) is a noun made to refer to the action of the verb. From a three lettered verb the *Ism Fael* (اسم الفاعل) is made in the form of *Fael* (فاعل)

كتب – كاتب، جلس – جالس، ذهب – ذاهب

نصر – ناصر، صدق – صادق

From more than three lettered word it is made from its present tense form by replacing the letter of present tense with mu (م) and giving *kasra* to the second last letter, e.g.:

أسلَمَ – يُسْلِمُ : مُسْلِمٌ ، أخرَجَ – يُخرْجُ : مُخرِجٌ، أنتَجَ – يُنْتِجُ : مُنتِجٌ

See the examples for three lettered and more than three lettered verbs used in sentences.

Three lettered verbs:

صَدَقَ الغُلامُ   فالغُلامُ صَادقٌ

نَدِمَ الظَّالِمُ   فالظالم نادم

غَرَسَ البُسْتَانِي الشَّجَرَةَ   فالبستاني غَارِسٌ

More than three lettered verbs:

أَتْقَنَ الصَّانِعُ العَمَلَ   فالعاملُ مُتقنٌ

استجَابَ الله الدُّعَاء   فاللهُ مُسْتَجِيبٌ

انتَجَ الصَّانِعُ   فالصَّانِعُ منتجٌ

اسم المفعول:

اسم المفعول اسم مصوغ للدلالة على ما وقع عليه فعل الفاعل وهو من الثلاثي على صورة مفعول ومن غير الثلاثي على صورة اسم فاعل مع فتح ما قبل الآخر.

Ism Mafool (اسم المفعول) is a noun made to refer to the action occurred on it from the doer. From a three lettered verb it is made in the form of مفعول and from more than three lettered verb in the same form of *ism fael* by giving *fatha* to the second last letter.

Examples for three lettered verbs:

فَتَحَ الخَادِمُ البَابَ   فالبابُ مفتوحٌ

شُرِبَ الحَلِيبُ   فالحَلِيبُ مشروبٌ

ضرب المعلم الولد   فالولد مَضرُوبٌ

From more than three lettered verbs:

أَكْرَمتُ الضَّيفَ   فالضَّيفُ مُكرَمٌ

عَاقَبَ الحَاكِمُ المُذنِبَ   فالمُذنِبُ مُعَاقَبٌ

تَعَمَّدَت السُّكُوت   فالسُّكُوتُ مُتَعَمَّدٌ

LESSON EIGHTEEN

THE NOMINATIVE CASES (المرفوعات)

> There are eight nominative cases in Arabic and they are:
>
> الفاعل، نائب الفاعل، المبتدأ، الخبر، اسم كان وأخواتها، خبر ان
>
> وأخواتها، اسم ما و لا مشابه بليس، خبر لا لنفي الجنس

Examples

1. The doer (الفاعل)

The boy wrote the lesson	كتب الولد الدرس
The child slept	نام الطفل
The man laughed	ضحك الرجل

Underlined words in these sentences are doers and hence in nominative cases.

2. Naib Fael (نائب الفاعل)

The soldier was killed	قتل الجندي
The door was opened	فتح الباب
The gold was stolen	سرق الذهب

In these examples the doers are not mentioned and the objects have taken the position of the doers. The object which takes the place of the doer when it is not mentioned is known as نائب الفاعل

3,4. The subject and the predicate (المبتدأ والخبر)

The boy is industrious	الوَلَدُ مُجْتَهِدٌ
The school is big	المَدرَسَةُ كَبِيرَةٌ
The examination is easy	الامتِحَانُ سَهْلٌ

In these examples the first words are subjects and the second words are predicates. The subjects and predicates of nominal sentences are nominative.

5. *Ism* of *kana* and her sisters (اسم كان وأخواتها)

تدخل كان على المبتدا والخبر فترفع الأول فيسمى اسمها وتنصب الثاني ويسمى خبرها. مثل كان فيما تقدم صار وليس وأصبح وأضحى وأصبح و أمسى و ظل و بات.

Kana enters in a nominal sentence and gives nominative case to the first noun and that will be known as noun of *kana*. The predicate will be given *nasb* and it will be known as predicate of *kana*.

The following words also do the action of *kana* and hence they are called the sisters of *kana*.

صار و ليس و أصبح وأضحى و أمسى و ظل وبات

Allah is the Most Forgiving	كَانَ اللهُ غَفُورًا
The boy became smart	صَارَ الوَلَدُ نَشِيطًا
The examination is not tough	لَيسَ الامتِحانُ صَعْبًا
The sinner became sad	أصْبَحَ المُجرِمُ نَادِمًا
The rose became faded	أضْحَى الوَرَدُ ذَابِلاً

The worker became tired (in the evening)	أَمْسَى العَامِلُ تَعْبَانًا
The patient spent the night crying	بَاتَ المَرِيضُ بَاكِيًا

6. Predicate of *inna* and her sisters (خبر ان وأخواتها)

Surely the examination is near	إنَّ الامْتِحَانَ قَرِيبٌ
Surely the boy is smart	إنَّ الوَلَدَ شَاطِرٌ
Surely the girl is beautiful	إنَّ البِنتَ جَمِيلَةٌ
Surely the hard working person is successful	إنَّ الرَّجُلَ المُجْتَهدَ نَاجِحٌ

7. Noun of *ma* and *la* similar to *laysa* (اسم ما و لا مشابه بليس)

Ma and *La* resemble to laysa are negative particles. When these letters come in the nominal sentence the first noun will be in the nominative case and the second noun will be in accusative case. *Ma* can be used before definite (معرفة) and indefinite (نكرة) nouns.

Khalid is not industrious	ما خالد مجتهدًا
Hamid is not smart	ما حامد شاطرًا
The room is not vast	ما الغُرفَةُ واسعةً

La will be used before indefinite nouns only

No house is rented	لا بيت مؤجرا
No boy is absent	لا ولد غائبًا
No flight is landing	لا طائرة مهبطة

8. Predicate of *la* used for the negation of collective nouns (خبر لا لنفي الجنس)

No student is standing	لا طالب قائم
No man is civilized	لا رجل مهذب
No room is vacant	لا غرفة خالية

LESSON NINETEEN

THE ACCUSATIVE CASES (المنصوبات)

There are 13 accusative cases. They are:

٢) المفعول به	١) المفعول المطلق
٤) المفعول لأجله	٣) المفعول له
٦) المفعول فيه	٥) المفعول معه
٨) التمييز،	٧) الحال
١٠) اسم ان وأخواتها	٩) المستثنى
١٢) خبر ما و لا مشابه بليس	١١) خبر كان وأخواتها
	١٣) اسم لا لنفي الجنس

١) المفعول المطلق

المفعول المطلق اسم منصوب موافق للفعل في لفظه ويجيئ بعد الفعل لتأكيده
ولبيان نوعه أو عدده

It is the infinite (مصدر) of the preceding verb and is used in three different ways.

Hasan played a game   لعب حسن لعبا

The tiger jumps lion's jump   يثب النمر وثوب الأسد

Ali ate twice   أكل علي أكلتين

٢) المفعول به

المفعول به اسم منصوب وقع عليه فعل الفاعل

The object is a noun in the accusative case on which the action of the doer takes place.

The boy wrote the lesson	كَتَبَ الوَلَدُ الدَّرْسَ
The girl read the newspaper	قَرَأَتْ البِنتُ الجَرِيدَةَ
The mother cooked the food	طَبَخَتْ الأُمُّ الطَّعَامَ

٣) المفعول له

The teacher beat the child for teaching him good manners	ضرب المعلم الوَلَدَ تَأْدِيبًا لَه
Hamid fought courageously	قَاتَلَ حَامِد شُجَاعَةً
I opened the door for ventilation	فَتَحْتُ البَابَ تَهوِيةً

٤) المفعول فيه (الظرف)

ظرف الزمان : اسم منصوب يبين الزمن الذي حصل فيه الفعل

ظرف المكان : اسم منصوب يبين المكان الذي حصل فيه الفعل

The patient drank medicine in the morning	شَرِبَ المَرِيضُ الدَّوَاءَ صَبَاحًا
I played under the tree	لَعِبْتُ تَحتَ الشَّجَرَة
I stayed in Saudi for a month	مكثتُ في السعودية شَهرًا
The craw flew above the tree	طَارَ الغُرابُ فَوقَ الشَجَرَة

٥) المفعول معه

The object referring to the accompaniment by adding واو المعية is called المفعول معه

I went to School with Khalid	ذَهَبتُ المَدرَسَةَ وخالدا
I traveled to Lebanon with Hamid	سَافرتُ الى لبنان وحامدا
Ahmad came with a servant	جاء احمد وخادمًا

٦) المفعول لأجله

المفعول لأجله اسم منصوب يبين سبب الفعل وعلة حصوله

A noun in the accusative case which explains the reason for the occurrence of the action.

Students travel to Europe in search of knowledge	يسافر الطلبة الى أوربا طلبا للعلم
The judge punished the sinner to teach him manners	عَاقَبَ القَاضي المجرمَ تأديبا له
Stand up in respect to your teacher	قُمْ احترَامًا لأستاذكَ

٧) الحال

الحال اسم منصوب يبين هيئة الفاعل أو المفعول به حين وقوع الفعل ويسمى كل من الفاعل أو المفعول به صاحب الحال.

It is a noun in the accusative case which explains the condition of the doer or the object or both of them at the time of the occurrence of the action. These doers and objects are called صاحب الحال.

The water flew pure	جَرَى المَاءُ صَافِيًا
The boy came crying	أقبل الوَلَدُ بَاكِيًا
Muhammad returned successfully	عَادَ محمد نَاجِحًا
Don't wear the dress which is dirty	لا تلبس الثوبَ وسْخًا
I bought the chair (that was) broken	اشتَرَيتُ الكُرسي مكسورًا

٨) التمييز

التمييز اسم يذكر لبيان المراد من اسم سابق يصلح لأن تراد به اشياء كثيرة التمييز قسمان: ملفوظ وملحوظ. فالأول ما يلفظ به في الجملة كأسماء الوزن والكيل والمسافة والعدد والثاني ما يفهم من الجملة من غير ان يذكر فيها

Tamyeez (Distinctive term) is a noun mentioned to clear the intention of the preceding noun , in the absence of which the idea will not be specific. Distinctive terms in Arabic grammar must be indefinite and should end with *tanween* in accusative.

I saw eleven stars	رَأَيتُ أَحَدَ عَشَرَ كَوكَبًا
They are forty students	هم أربعُونَ طَالبًا
How much money have you got?	كم مالاً عندَكَ
He is elder than you	هو أكبرُ منكَ سنًّا
I have got fifty rupees	عندي خمسون روبيةً
I have got more money than you	أنا أكثرُ منكَ مالاً
My Lord, increase my knowledge	رب زِدْني علمًا

المستثنى بإلا

يسمى الاسم الذي يقع بعد الا مستثنى. ويسمى الاسم الذي يجيئ قبلها

ويشتمل في المعنى على ما بعدها مستثنى منه

المستثنى بالا اسم يذكر بعدها مخالفا في الحكم لما قبلها

Friends came except Ali	جَاءَ الأصدقَاءُ إلا عَلِيًّا
I read the whole book except two pages	قرأتُ الكتابَ إلا صَفْحَتَينِ
I solved the all accounts problems except one	حَلَلتُ مَسائلَ الحسابِ إلا مَسألةً

حكم المستثنى بإلا

• إذا كان المستثنى منه مذكورا وكان الكلام مثبتا وجب نصب المستثنى بإلا.

أثمرَت الأشجارُ الا شَجَرةً

طَارَ الْحَمامُ الا واحدةً

فَرَّ الجُنُودُ الا القائدَ

• إذا كان المستثنى منه مذكورا وكان الكلام منفيا جاز في المستثنى بالا ان

ينصب على الاستثناء وان يتبع المستثنى منه في اعرابه.

لم تَفتَحَ الأزهارُ الا البنفسجَ (البنفسج)

لم ينج المستحمون الا أحمد (أحمد)

• اذا كان المستثنى منه محذوفا اعرب المستثنى على حسب ما يقتضيه موضعه

في التركيب كما لو كانت الا غير موجودة.

ما صاحَبتُ الا الأخيار

اسم ان وأخواتها

خبر كان وأخواتها

خبر ما و لا مشابه بليس

اسم لا لنفي الجنس

LESSON TWENTY

PRONOUNS الضمائر

الضمير اسم معرفة يدل على المتكلم أو المخاطب أو الغائب

Pronoun is a known noun referring to the first, second or third person.

I will not be late in the morning	أنا لا أتأخَّرُ في الصَّباحِ
We know the duty	نحن نَعرِفُ الوَاجبَ
You love the country	أنتَ تُحبُّ الوَطَنَ
You obey the teacher	أنتِ تطيعينَ المُعلِّمة
The teacher did not honour except you	ما اكرم المعلم الا اياك
He is interested in game	هُوَ مولع باللعب

Explanation :

Think about the words أنا ، نحن ، أنتَ ، إياك ، هو in the examples given. You can see they all are nouns referring to certain specific things known to us. So they are known nouns. If you observe closely you can see that some of them are referring to first person, some others to second person and the remaining to third persons. Known nouns of these kinds referring to first person, second person or third persons are known as pronouns.

Exercises

1. Find out pronouns known to you from the following sentences

أنتَ تأمُرُ ونَحنُ نُطيعُ. أنتم رِجالُ الغدِ.

الزُّرَّاعُ والصُّنَّاعُ هُم أسَاسُ الثَّروةِ.

الشَّمسُ والقَمرُ هُما الْمَصدرُ الأكبرُ للضياءِ.

2. Put appropriate pronouns in the beginning of the following sentences

أقومُ منَ النَّومِ مُبَكِّرًا. تَمشُطُ شَعرَهَا كلَّ يَومٍ.

يُساعدُونَ الفُقَرَاءَ. تَشكُرُ مَن يُسَاعدُكَ .

تَتَّبِعينَ قَواعدَ الصحَّةَ. نُكرِمُ الضَيفَ.

3. Put suitable pronouns in place of proper nouns in the sentences

عليٌ يُصيدُ السَّمَكَ. الحسنانِ زارا حديقة الحيوانات.

المحمدون يستحمون في النهر.

Answers

I. ١) أنت / نحن ٢) هُما ٣) هم (٤) انتم

II. ١) أنا ٢) هي ٣) هم (٤) أنت ٥) أنت ٦) نحن

III. ١) هُو ٢) هُما ٣) هُم

LESSON TWENTY ONE

VARIOUS TYPES OF PRONOUNS

Pronouns can be divided into three types:

Separate (detached) pronoun الضمير المنفصل

Attached pronouns الضمير المتصل

Hidden pronouns الضمير المستتر

Separate (detached) pronoun الضمير المنفصل

الضمير المنفصل ما يمكن النطق به وحده من غير ان يتصل بكلمة
أخرى

Separate pronouns are those pronouns that can be pronounced alone without being added to any other words.

Examples

I am a listener	أنا سَامِعٌ
We are obedient	نَحْنُ مُطِيعُونَ
You are hard-working	أنتَ مُجتَهِدٌ
You are neat	انتِ نَظِيفَةٌ
He is an engineer	هُوَ مُهَندِسٌ

She is civilized	هِيَ مُهَذَّبَةٌ
The teacher praised me alone.	إِيَّايَ مَدَحَ المُدَرِّسُ
Thee (Allah) alone we worship	إِيَّاكَ نَعْبُدُ

Explanation

Analyse these examples then you can see that all the pronouns used in these examples (أنا ، نحن ، أنت ، أنتِ ، هو ، هي ، إياي ، إياك) can be pronounced alone.

If you observe these examples again you can see the pronouns أنا ، نحن ، أنت ، أنتِ ، هو ، هي have come as subject and subject is grammatically nominative. But as the particles are *mabnee* (مبني) we can find the symbol of nominative case on the pronouns. But we can say that they are in place of nominative cases.

But in the last two examples إياي ، إياك have come as objects and object is always accusative.

From this we can understand that there are certain pronouns specially for nominative cases and some others exclusively for accusative cases.

Detached pronouns exclusively for nominative cases are:

First person singular	أنا
First person plural	نحن
Second person masculine singular	أنتَ
Second person feminine singular	أنتِ
Second person masculine+ feminine dual	أنتما
Second person masculine plural	أنتم

Second person feminine plural	أنتن
Third person masculine singular	هو
Third person feminine singular	هي
Third person masculine+ feminine dual	هما
Third person masculine plural	هم
Third person feminine plural	هن

Detached pronouns exclusively for accusative cases are:

First person singular	إياي
First person plural	إيانا
Second person masculine singular	إياك
Second person feminine singular	إياك
Second person masculine+ feminine dual	إياكما
Second person masculine plural	إياكم
Second person meminine plural	إياكن
Third person masculine singular	إياه
Third person feminine singular	إياها
Third person masculine+ feminine dual	إياهما
Third person masculine plural	إياهم
Third person feminine plural	إياهن

Exercise

Make the following nouns predicates of suitable detached pronouns

نظيف	مهذبان	مطيعة
محسنات	نشيطتان	كرماء

73

Answer

أنتَ نَظيفٌ   هُمَا مُهذَّبَان   أنتِ مُطيعَةٌ

هُنَ مُحْسِنَاتٌ   أنْتُمَا نَشيطَتَان   أنْتُم كُرَمَاء

Attached Pronouns الضمير المتصل

الضمير المتصل هو الذي لا ينطق به وحده ويتصل دائما بكلمة أخرى

Attached pronouns are those pronouns that can't be pronounced alone and come always attached to another word.

Examples

I traveled to Saudi.	سَافَرتُ إلى السعودية.
We went to the ground.	ذَهبنا إلى الملعَب.
They (two male) went to the school.	ذهبا إلى المَدرَسَة.
You (many male) write the lesson.	اكتُبوا الدَّرسَ.
You (a female) clean the house.	نَظفي البيتَ.
Mothers civilize their children.	الأُمَّهَاتُ يُهذبنَ أوْلادَهُنَ.
My brother's advise benefited me.	نَفَعَني نَصح أخي.
Your teacher gave you a book.	أعطاكَ معلمكَ كتابًا.
Hasan's brother loves him.	حَسَن يُحبُهُ أخوهُ.
Our hard work benefited us.	أفادَنَا اجْتِهَادُنَا.
Ali took a letter from me.	أخَذَ عَلي منِّي رسَالةً.
We have a house with a garden in it.	لنا منزل به حديقة.

Explanation :

In the first six examples all sentences carry a pronoun each referring to first person, second person or third person.

The last six examples carry two pronouns each. But all these pronouns are attached to other words and we are unable to read them alone. That is why they are called attached pronouns.

If you analyse the examples closely you can see that the pronouns in the first six examples have come in the place of doer and doer is always nominative.

الضمائر المتصلة بالافعال وهي خاصة بالرفع هي التاء والف الاثنين و واو الجماعة وياء المخاطبة ونون النسوة

Attached pronouns with verbs that are special to nominative cases are :

Ta, alif referring to dual, *waw* referring to masculine plural, *ya* referring to second person feminine singular and *noon* referring to feminine plural.

The first six examples explained earlier give clear indications to this effect.

ياء المتكلم وكاف المخاطب وهاء الغائب اذا اتصلت بالافعال كانت في محل نصب واذا اتصلت بالاسماء او حروف الجر كانت في محل جر.

ياء of first person ك of second person and of third person, if they are attached to verbs they will be in place of accusative case and if they are attached to nouns or letters of genitive cases then they will be in genitive case.

الضمير نا يكون مرة في محل رفع ومرة في محل نصب ومرة في محل جر.

The pronoun نا can be in nominative, accusative and genitive cases.

The hidden pronoun الضمير المستتر

> الضمير المستتر هو ضمير اتصل بالفعل من غير أن يظهر في اللفظ.
>
> Hidden pronouns are pronouns that are attached to verbs without being seen in the word.

The boy played	الوَلَدَ لَعِبَ
The girl sang	البِنتُ انشَدَتْ

الضمير المستتر في الفعل الماضي تقديره هو أو هي

The hidden pronouns in the past tense will be he (هو) or she (هي).

I want you to work hard	أُرِيدُ أَنْ تَجتَهِدَ
Indeed we like your success	انَّنَا نُحبُّ نَجَاحَكَ

الضمير المستتر في الفعل المضارع يختلف تقديره باختلاف حروف المضارعة

The hidden pronouns assumed in present tense varry according to the letters of present tense.

Teacher teaches	المُعَلِمُ يُدَرِّسُ
Mother cleans the house	الأمُّ تُنَظِفُ البَيتَ

الضمير المستتر في فعل الأمر تقديره أنت دائما

Hidden pronouns assumed in imperative verbs will be always انت

Clean your teeth	نَظِّفْ أَسْنَانَكَ
Respect the elder	احْتَرِمْ الكَبِيرَ

Explanation :

Observe the examples and find out the doers of these verbs. We can see doers in all these examples are pronouns that are not seen. So they are called hidden pronouns.

In the first example doer is the pronoun هو and in the second example it is هي

You can find out the doers in the remaining examples based on the explanation given.

Exercises:

1. Assume hidden pronouns in the following sentences

١) الشُّرْطِيُّ يَقْبِضُ عَلَى اللِّصِّ.

٢) السَّاعَةُ دَقَّتْ ثَلاَثًا.

٣) أَنْجِزْ الوَعْدَ.

٤) نَحْنُ نَرْفَعُ شَأْنَ مَدْرَسَتِنَا.

٥) زَيْنَب تُجِيدُ الطَّبْخَ.

٦) أُحِبُّ النَّيْلَ.

٧) لا تَشْرَبْ وَأَنْتَ تَعْبَان.

٨) القِطَارُ قَدِمَ فِي مَوعِدِهِ.

2. Change the past tense in the following sentences into present tense and identify the doer in each one.

١) سَمِعْتُ النِّدَاءَ.

٢) ذَهَبْنَا الَى المنزِلِ.

٤) تُرَتِّب دُرْجَكَ.

٥) العُصْفُورُ طَارَ مِنَ القَفَصِ.

٦) الدَّجَاجَةُ بَاضَتْ.

٧) وَدَّعْنَا المُسَافِرَ.

Answers :

I.

٤) نحن	٣) أنت	٢) هي	١) هو
٨) هو	٧) أنت	٦) أنا	٥) هي

II.

٣) أنت	٢) نحن	١) انا
٦) نحن	٥) هي	٤) هو

LESSON TWENTY TWO

CLASSIFICATION OF NOUN INTO SINGULAR, DUAL AND PLURAL
تقسيم الاسم الى مفرد ومثنى وجمع

الاسم يَنْقَسِمُ إلى ثَلاثَة أقسَام : مُفْرَد وَمُثَنَّى وجَمْع

المُفْرَدُ: مَا دَلَّ عَلَى شَيْءٍ وَاحِدٍ.

الْمثنى: ما دل على شيئين اثنين بزيادة الف ونون أو ياء ونون في آخره.

الْجمع: ما دلَّ عَلَى أكثر من اثنين.

Nouns can be divided into singular, dual and plural.
Singular: Word referring to one.

Dual: Word referring to two by adding *alif* and *noon* in nominative case and *ya* and *noon* in accusative and genitive cases.

Plural: Word referring to more than two.

E.g.:

المفرد :

The worker became tired.	تَعِبَ العَامِلُ.
The engineer came.	حَضَرَ المُهَنْدِسُ.

I called the seller.	نَادَيْتُ الْبَائِعَ.
I praised the civilised (girl).	أَثْنَيْتُ على الْمُهَذَّبة.

الْمُثنى:

Two workers became tired.	تَعِبَ العَامِلان.
Two engineers came.	حضر المهندسان.
I called two sellers.	نادَيتُ البائعين.
I praised two civilized (girls).	أثنيتُ على المهذبتَين.

الجمع:

The workers became tired.	تعب العمال.
The engineers came.	حضر المهندسون.
I called the sellers.	ناديت البائعينَ.
I praised the civilized (girls).	أثنيت على المهذبات.

See the given examples. In the first four examples we find singular nouns are used. In the second four examples the nouns are dual and in the last four examples the nouns are plurals.

Exercise :

1. Identify the singular, dual and plural nouns from the following passage.

ذَهَبْتُ مَرَّةً لِزِيَارَة صَدِيق. فَأَدْخَلَني في حُجْرَة لَهَا ثَلاَثَةُ شَبَابيكَ وَبَابَان. جُدْرَانُهَا مُزَيَّنَةٌ بالصُّوَر والرُّسُوم وأرْضُهَا مَفْرُوشَةٌ بالبَسْط الفَارسِيَّة وَفِيهَا أَرَائكُ مصفُوفَةٌ وفي أحَد جَوَانبهَا خَزَانَةُ كُتُب عَجيبة وَرَأيتُ هُنَاكَ رَجُلَيْنِ جَالِسَين يَذْكُرَان أَخْبَارَ الْمُخْتَرعينَ ويَقُصَّان مَا يشوق المستمعين من الحكايات اللطيفة والنوادر الطريفة.

80

2. Make dual form of the following nouns :

باب	شجرة	طريق	عصفور	كريم
كتاب	ذكي	حديقة	نمر	ورقة

3. Make the singular of the following nouns:

نجوم	بساتين	مؤمنات	بحار	سفن
حجرات	فنادق	جنود	أطباء	مخترعون

Answers

1.

جمع	مثنى	مفرد
شبابيك	بابان	صديق
جدران	رجلين	حجرة
صور	جالسين	أرض
رسوم، أرائك،		خزانة
جوانب، كتب، أخبار،		بسط
المخترعين، مستمعين،		
حكايات، نوادر		

2.

مثنى	مفرد
بابان	باب
شجرتان	شجرة
طريقان	طريق
عصفوران	عصفور

كريم	كريمان
ذكي	ذكيان
حديقة	حديقتان
فهر	فهران
كتاب	كتابان
ورقة	ورقتان

جمع	مفرد
نجوم	نجم
بساتين	بستان
مؤمنات	مؤمنة
بحار	بحر
سفن	سفينة
حجرات	حجرة
فنادق	فندق
جنود	جند
أطباء	طبيب
مخترعون	مخترع

CONDITIONS OF THE DUAL اعراب المثنى

يرفع المثنى بالالف وينصب ويجر بالياء

Dual will get nominative case with *alif* and accusative and genitive cases with *ya*

E.g:

Two boys played.	لَعِبَ الوَلَدَان.
Two partners agreed.	اتَّفَقَ الشَّرِيكَان.
Two travelers came.	حَضَرَ المُسَافِرَان.
I taught two boys.	عَلَّمتُ الوَلَدَينِ.
I spoke to two partners.	حادثت الشَّرِيكَينِ.
I treated two travelers.	عَالَجتُ المُسَافِرَينِ.
I gave the ball to two boys.	أعطيتُ الكُرَةَ للوَلَدَينِ.
I bought from two partners.	اشتَرَيتُ مِنَ الشَّرِيكَينِ.
I greeted with Salam two travelers.	سَلمتُ عَلَى المُسَافِرَينِ.

Explanation :

Observe the examples and see the last words in all these examples are dual nouns. They are in the nominative cases in the first three examples as they are doers. In the second three they are in accusative cases as they are objects and in the last three examples they are in genitive cases as they are preceded by letters of *jarr*. But see what is the symbol of nominative, accusative and genitive cases in these examples? Then you can understand that they all end with alif and noon in nominative cases and with *ya* and noon in accusative and genitive cases. From this observation we come to the conclusion that the dual will get nominative case with *alif* and *noon* as accusative and genitive cases will be with *ya* and *noon*.

Exercise:

1. Identify the dual in nominative, accusative and genitive cases in the following sentences and mention the reason for that:

الْبَابَانِ مفتُوحَان. يَجُرُّ الْمِحْرَاثَ ثَوْرَان. تَمشِى الدَّجَاجَةُ عَلَى رِجلَينِ. كَانَتِ الْحُجْرَتَانِ ضَيِّقَتَينِ. اَكَلتُ تُفَاحَتَينِ. قَرَأتُ مِنَ الكِتَابِ صَفحَتَينِ. اشتريتُ الكِتَابَ بِقِرشَينِ. انَ الكَبشَينِ سَمِينَانِ.

2. Use the dual form of the following nouns in sentences

بائع	صورة	كرسي	غرفة	عمود
المدرسة	البقرة	السفينة	كتاب	قلم

Answers :

1.

مبتدأ	–	مرفوع	–	البابان
خبر	–	مرفوع	–	مفتوحان
فاعل	–	مرفوع	–	ثوران
سبقه على	–	مجرور	–	رجلين

اسم كان	–	مرفوع	–	الحجرتان
خبر كان	–	منصوب	–	ضيقتين
مفعول به	–	منصوب	–	تفاحتين
مفعول به	–	منصوب	–	صفحتين
سبقه ب	–	مجرور	–	بقرتين
اسم ان	–	منصوب	–	كبشين
خبر ان	–	مرفوع	–	سمينتان

3.

الغرفتان واسعتان.	هذان العمودان قويان.
الصورتان جديدتان.	الكرسيان مكسوران.
اشتريت قلمين.	البائعان صديقان.
السفينتان قديمتان.	قرأت كتابين.
المدرستان كبيرتان.	البقرتان سمينتان.

LESSON TWENTY FOUR

THE PLURAL الجمع

ينقسم الجمع الى ثلاثة أقسام:

جمع التكسير وجمع مذكر السالم وجمع مؤنث السالم

جمع التكسير/الكسرة: ما دل على أكثر من اثنين بتغيير صورة مفرده.

جمع مذكر السالم : ما دل على أكثر من اثنين بزيادة واو ونون او ياء ونون في آخره.

جمع المؤنث السالم: ما دل على أكثر من اثنتين بزيادة الف وتاء في آخره

Plurals can be divided into three

Broken Plural: Word referring to more than two and made by changing the structure of its singular.

Sound Masculine Plural: Referring to more than two (masculine nouns) by adding *wa* and noon or *yae* and *noon* at the end.

Sound Feminine Plural: Nouns referring to more than two (feminine nouns) by adding *alif* and *ta* at the end.

Eg:

Men came	جاء الرجال
I read books	قرأت الكتب
I walked with men	مشيت مع الرجال
The Muslims succeeded	فاز المسلمون
I honoured the Muslims	أكرمت المسلمين
I said salam to the Muslims	سلمت على المسلمين
Hard-working (girls) succeeded	فازت المجتهدات
I honored hard-working (girls)	أكرمت المجتهدات
I said salam to hard working (girls)	سلمت على المجتهدات

Observe the examples given. You can see all the sentences consist plural nouns. In the first three examples the plural noun is made by breaking the singular. But in the next three examples also we find plurals. The difference here is these plurals are referring to masculine things and these are made by adding some letters at the end of its singular. What are these letters added to form plurals?. If you analyse this seriously you can see that we are adding *wa* and *noon* at the end when it is in nominative case and *ya* and *noon* at the end in accusative and genitive cases.

Now observe the last three examples. These words are referring to feminine nouns. The plurals in these examples are also made by adding some letters at the end of its singular without making any changes to the basic structure of its singular. The letters added are *alif* and *ta*

Sound Masculine Plural جمع مذكر السالم

جمع مذكر السالم يرفع بالواو وينصب ويجر الياء

Sound Masculine Plural will have *waw* in nominative case and *ya* in accusative and genitive cases,e.g.:

The travellers came	جاء المسافرون
The Muslims went	ذهب المسلمون
The hard workers succeeded	نجح المجتهدون
I am feeding the travelers	أطعم المسافرين
We love hard workers	نحب المجتهدين
We encourage the winners	نشجع الفائزين
We wish good for the hard workers	نرجو الخير للمجتهدين
We praise the winners	نثني على الفائزين
We look to the players.	ننظر الى اللاعبين

Explanation:

In the first three examples the plurals have come as doers and they are in nominative cases. That is why we find *wa* and *noon* at the end..

In the second three examples , they are in accusative cases as they are objects and in the last three examples they are in genitive cases as they are preceded by letters of *jarr*. In both these cases we find Sound Masculine Plurals are ending with *ya* and *noon*.

Sound Feminine Plural جمع المؤنث السالم

جمع مؤنث السالم يرفع بالضمة وينصب ويجر بالكسرة

Sound Feminine Plural will get nominative case with *Dammu* and accusative and genitive cases with *Kasra*, e.g.:

The Muslim (women) came	جاءت المسلمات
Good ladies succeeded	نجحت الصالحات
The tress grew	نمت الشجرات
I slaughtered chicken	ذبحت الدجاجات
I praised the Muslim (women)	مدحت المسلمات
I cut the tress	قطعت الشجرات
I said salam to the Muslim women	سلمت على المسلمات
I climbed on the trees	صعدت على الشجرات

The boy fell down from the trees. سقط الولد من الشجرات

See the last words of the examples given. You can see that all of them are Sound Feminine Plurals. Now think about the grammatical position of each one of them.

In the first three examples they have come as doers and doers are always nominative. Here you can note that the last letters carry *damma* as the symbol of nominative case.

In the second three examples the plurals have come as objects and objects are accusative. But we find the last letters have got *Kasra*. From this we reach a conclusion that Sound Feminine Plural will get accusative with *Kasra* only.

Now observe the last three examples. There are also Sound Feminine Plurals in each example and they all are preceded by letters of *jarr*. We can see *Kasra* at the end of the noun and we say Sound Feminine Plural will get *jarr* with *Kasra*.

LESSON TWENTY FIVE

CONJUNCTIONS العطف

العطف تابع يتوسط بينه وبين متبوعه أحد هذه الحروف وهي:
الواو والفاء وثم و أو و أم و لا و بل ولكن وحتى

الامثلة:

أكلت الأنبج والعنب.   نضج الأنبج والعنب.

ترعد السماء وتبرق.   هذا شجر الأنبج والعنب.

يخاف الأطفال من ان ترعد السماء وتبرق.

ان ترعد السماء وتبرق فلن تخرج.

If you observe these examples you can understand that these sentences have two parts and there is a *waw* between them denoting that they share the sense of the action. In the first three examples these words are nouns and in the last three examples they are verbs. The word after *wa* is called *matoof* (معطوف) and *waw* is called letter of *atf* (حرف العطف)

Meaning of the letters of conjunction معاني حروف العطف

حروف العطف تسعة: الواو وهي لمطلق الجمع والفاء للترتيب مع التعقيب وثم للترتيب مع التراخي و أو للشك أو التخيير و أم لطلب التعيين ولا للنفي وبل للاخراب ولكن للاستدراك وحتى للغاية.

Instead of giving more explanation on this I would give certain examples that are self explanatory.

صلى الامام والماموم.	تولى الخلافة أبو بكر و عمر.
حكم مصر اسماعيل فتوفيق.	دخل المدرس فوقف التلاميذ.
مات الرشيد ثم المأمون.	رأينا أبوك فحيانا.
خذ وردا أو بنفسجا.	زرعنا القطن ثم جنيناه.
أ تفاحا أكلت أم برتقالا؟	نقل الخبر علي أو فريد.
اشتريت دواة بل قلما.	حصدنا القمح لا الشعير.
فر الجنود حتى القائد.	ما جاء السيد لكن خادمه.

PART TWO

TRANSLATION

THE TRANSLATION

Do you go to school every day?	هَلْ تَذْهَبُ إِلَى الْمَدْرَسَةِ كُلَّ يَوْمٍ؟	١)
This boy has passed the exam	قَدْ نَجَحَ هَذَا الْوَلَدُ فِي الْامْتِحَانِ	٢)
You are an intelligent boy	أَنْتَ وَلَدٌ ذَكِيٌّ	٣)
She is a smart girl	هِيَ بِنْتٌ شَاطِرَةٌ	٤)
How did you reach school?	كَيْفَ وَصَلْتَ الْمَدْرَسَةَ؟	٥)
My friend has returned from India	قَدْ رَجَعَ صَدِيقِي مِنَ الْهِنْدِ	٦)
These birds are very small.	هَذِهِ الطُّيُوْرُ صَغِيرَةٌ جِدًّا	٧)
The train was very fast	كَانَ الْقِطَارُ سَرِيْعًا جِدًّا	٨)
I am angry today	أَنَا زَعْلَانُ الْيَوْمَ	٩)
He is tired now	هُوَ تَعْبَانٌ الْحِيْنِ	١٠)
I love my country very much	أُحِبُّ بَلَدِيْ جِدًّا	١١)
Have you got a text book, a pen and a note book?	هَلْ عِنْدَكَ كِتَابٌ وَقَلَمٌ وَكُرَّاسَةٌ ؟	١٢)
Don't play (M.Plural) in the class	لَا تَلْعَبُوْا فِي الْفَصْلِ	١٣)
He wants to travel to Delhi	يُرِيدُ أَنْ يُسَافِرَ إِلَى دَلْهِي	١٤)
My friend told me	قَالَ لِي صَدِيقِي	١٥)
Do you like to read this book?	هَلْ تُحِبُّ أَنْ تَقْرَأَ هَذَا الْكِتَابَ	١٦)
Our school is in New Delhi	مَدْرَسَتُنَا فِي دَلْهِي الْجَدِيْدَةِ	١٧)

His examination starts tomorrow	١٨) يَبْدَأُ امْتِحَانُهُ غَدًا
Book is a very good friend	١٩) اَلْكِتَاب صَدِيقٌ جَيِّدٌ جِدًّا
Railway station is near to his house	٢٠) مَحَطَّةُ الْقِطَارِ قَرِيبٌ مِن بَيْتِهِ
How many books has your friend got?	٢١) كَمْ كِتَابًا عِنْدَ صَدِيْقِكَ ؟
What profession will you opt after the exam?	٢٢) أَيَّ مِهْنَةٍ تَخْتَارُ بَعْدَ الامْتِحَانِ؟
A lazy student will never succeed	٢٣) لَنْ يَنْجَحَ الطَّالِبُ الْكَسْلاَنُ
Where is your shop in the city?	٢٤) أَيْنَ دُكَّانُكُمْ فِي الْمَدِيْنَةِ؟
My brother and sister have read two books	٢٥) قَرَأَ أَخِي وَأُخْتِي كِتَابَيْنِ
How many trees are there in this garden?	٢٦) كَمْ شَجَرَةً فِي هَذِهِ الْحَدِيْقَةِ؟
The reward of truth is good	٢٧) جَزَاءُ الْحَقِّ حَسَنٌ
Water is necessary for life	٢٨) اَلْمَاءُ ضَرُوْرِيٌّ لِلْحَيَاةِ
Ahmed and Khalid went to the market	٢٩) ذَهَبَ أَحْمَدُ وَخَالِدٌ إِلَى السُّوقِ
Your shop is very far	٣٠) دُكَّانُكُمْ بَعِيْدٌ جِدًّا
Have you seen a train?	٣١) هَلْ رَأَيْتُمْ الْقِطَارَ؟
How many rooms are there in your house?	٣٢) كَمْ غُرْفَةً فِي بَيْتِكُمْ؟
Where is your house in the village?	٣٣) أَيْنَ بَيْتُكُمْ فِي الْقَرْيَةِ؟
Do you know Arabic?	٣٤) هَلْ تَعْرِفُ اللُّغَةَ الْعَرَبِيَّةَ؟

Do you speak Arabic?	٣٥) هَلْ تَتَكَلَّمُ اللُّغَةَ الْعَرَبِيَّةَ؟
Did you read the newspaper	٣٦) هَلْ قَرَأْتَ الْجَرِيْدَةَ؟
Yes I read it every day	٣٧) نَعَمْ أَقْرَأُهَا كُلَّ يَوْمٍ
Which newspaper do you read?	٣٨) أَيَّ جَرِيْدَةٍ تَقْرَأُ؟
The student is industrious	٣٩) اَلطَّالِبُ مُجْتَهِدٌ
They came to visit their uncle	٤٠) جَاءُوْا لِزِيَارَةِ عَمِّهِمْ
Your watch is cheap	٤١) سَاعَتُكَ رَخِيْصَةٌ
His car is expensive	٤٢) سَيَّارَتُهُ غَالِيَةٌ
Her house is new	٤٣) بَيْتُهَا جَدِيدٌ
Our school is big	٤٤) مَدْرَسَتُنَا كَبِيرَةٌ
My son is tall	٤٥) اِبْنِي طَوِيلٌ
His daughter is short	٤٦) اِبْنَتُهُ قَصِيرَةٌ
Her bag is heavy	٤٧) شَنْطَتُهَا ثَقِيْلَةٌ
His bag is light	٤٨) شَنْطَتُهُ خَفِيْفَةٌ
My house is small	٤٩) بَيْتِي صَغِيرٌ
His pen is old	٥٠) قَلَمُهُ قَدِيْمٌ
You are going to the school	٥١) تَذْهَبُوْنَ إِلَى الْمَدْرَسَةِ
My brother did not open the door	٥٢) لَمْ يَفْتَحْ أَخِي الْبَابَ
How many hours does your brother read at home?	٥٣) كَمْ سَاعَةً يَقْرَأُ أَخُوْكَ فِي الْبَيْتِ
How do you write this name?	٥٤) كَيْفَ تَكْتُبُ هَذَا الاِسْمَ ؟

Where is your house?	(٥٥) أَيْنَ بَيْتُكَ؟
Where is your school?	(٥٦) أَيْنَ مَدْرَسَتُكَ؟
Where is your car?	(٥٧) أَيْنَ سَيَّارَتُكَ؟
Where is your brother?	(٥٨) أَيْنَ أَخُوكَ؟
Where is your sister?	(٥٩) أَيْنَ أُخْتُكَ؟
Where is your principal?	(٦٠) أَيْنَ مُدِيرُكَ؟
They (M.Plural) want two books	(٦١) يُرِيدُونَ كِتَابَيْنِ
We shall go to the market after prayer	(٦٢) سَنَذْهَبُ إِلَى السُّوقِ بَعْدَ الصَّلَاةِ
Don't (M.Plural) play in this ground	(٦٣) لَا تَلْعَبُوا فِي هَذَا الْمَيْدَانِ
My school is in the old city	(٦٤) مَدْرَسَتِي فِي الْمَدِينَةِ الْقَدِيمَةِ
His book is on the table	(٦٥) كِتَابُهُ عَلَى الطَّاوِلَةِ
When will your father return from Kuwait?	(٦٦) مَتَى يَعُوْدُ أَبُوكَ مِنَ الْكُوَيْتِ؟
They (M.Dual) are intelligent students	(٦٧) هُمَا طَالِبَانِ ذَكِيَّانِ
Ahmed is the tallest boy in the class	(٦٨) أَحْمَدُ أَطْوَلُ طَالِبٍ فِي الْفَصْلِ؟
Faisal did not write the answers because his pen is broken.	(٦٩) مَا كَتَبَ فَيْصَلٌ الْأَجْوِبَةَ لِأَنَّ قَلَمَهُ مَكْسُورٌ
My teacher is a great scholar	(٧٠) مُدَرِّسِي عَالِمٌ جَلِيلٌ
The sun rise in the east	(٧١) تَطْلُعُ الشَّمْسُ مِنَ الْمَشْرِقِ

You are an intelligent and industrious student	أَنْتَ طَالِبٌ ذَكِيٌّ وَمُجْتَهِدٌ	(٧٢)
There are Rs.100 in my pocket	هُنَاكَ مِائَةُ رُوبِيَّةٍ فِي جَيْبِي	(٧٣)
How many brothers have you got?	كَمْ أَخًا لَكَ؟	(٧٤)
How many sisters have you got?	كَمْ أُخْتًا لَكَ؟	(٧٥)
The Quran is the Book of Allah	اَلْقُرْآنُ كِتَابُ اللهِ	(٧٦)
The principal is in his room	اَلْمُدِيرُ فِي غُرْفَتِهِ	(٧٧)
My father is a teacher in this school	أَبِي مُدَرِّسٌ فِي هَذِهِ الْمَدْرَسَةِ	(٧٨)
His brother is an engineer in that company	أَخُوهُ مُهَنْدِسٌ فِي تِلْكَ الشَّرِكَةِ	(٧٩)
Your mother is a doctor in this hospital	أُمُّكَ طَبِيبَةٌ فِيْ هَذَا الْمُسْتَشْفَى	(٨٠)
Don't enter this room (to a man)	لَا تَدْخُلْ هَذِهِ الْغُرْفَةَ	(٨١)
His sister is a nurse in that clinic	أُخْتُهُ مُمَرِّضَةٌ فِي تِلْكَ الْعِيَادَةِ	(٨٢)
Don't play in this ground (to a girl)	لَا تَلْعَبِي فِي هَذَا الْمَلْعَبِ	(٨٣)
You have three pens	عِنْدَكَ ثَلَاثَةُ أَقْلَامٍ	(٨٤)
He has five books	عِنْدَهُ خَمْسَةُ كُتُبٍ	(٨٥)
I have two books and three pens	عِنْدِي كِتَابَانِ وَثَلَاثَةُ أَقْلَامٍ	(٨٦)
This short lady is a nurse	هَذِهِ الْمَرْأَةُ الْقَصِيرَةُ مُمَرِّضَةٌ	(٨٧)
That tall man is an engineer	ذَلِكَ الرَّجُلُ الطَّوِيلُ مُهَنْدِسٌ	(٨٨)
I am a new student	أَنَا طَالِبٌ جَدِيدٌ	(٨٩)

I go to school every day	٩٠) أَذْهَبُ إِلَى اَلْمَدْرَسَةِ كُلَّ يَوْمٍ
He is an old teacher	٩١) هُوَ مُعَلِّمٌ قَدِيمٌ
I go with my father	٩٢) اَرُوحُ مَعَ أَبِي
How do you go home?	٩٣) كَيْفَ تَرُوحُ الْبَيْتَ؟
The new book is on the table	٩٤) اَلْكِتَابُ الْجَدِيدُ عَلَى الطَّاوِلَةِ
The new students went out of the class	٩٥) خَرَجَ الطُّلَّابُ الْجُدُدُ مِنَ الْفَصْلِ
The garden is beautiful	٩٦) اَلْبُسْتَانُ جَمِيلٌ
Who is the lady who went out of the house now?	٩٧) مَنِ السَّيِّدَةُ الَّتِي خَرَجَتْ مِنَ الْبَيْتِ الآنَ؟
The book, which is on the table, belongs to the teacher.	٩٨) اَلْكِتَابُ الَّذِي عَلَى الْمَكْتَبِ لِلْمُدَرِّسِ
The teacher's name is Hamid. What is the name of the engineer?	٩٩) اِسْمُ الْمُدَرِّسِ حَامِدٌ. مَا اِسْمُ الْمُهَنْدِسِ؟
Mohammed's son is in the class. Where is Hassan's son?	١٠٠) اِبْنُ مُحَمَّدٍ فِي الْفَصْلِ. اَيْنَ اِبْنُ حَسَنٍ؟
The shop belongs to the merchant	١٠١) اَلدُّكَّانُ لِلتَّاجِرِ
Have you got a book? No I don't have a book	١٠٢) أَعِنْدَكَ كِتَابٌ؟ لاَ مَا عِنْدِي كِتَابٌ
These are new books. They have just arrived from Delhi	١٠٣) هَذِهِ كُتُبٌ جَدِيدَةٌ هِيَ وَصَلَتْ الآنَ مِنْ دَلْهِي
The Arabs are generous	١٠٤) اَلشَّعْبُ الْعَرَبِيُّ كَرِيمٌ

It rains from the sky	١٠٥) يَنْزِلُ الْمَطَرُ مِنَ السَّمَاءِ
Khalid rode on the bicycle	١٠٦) رَكِبَ خَالِدٌ عَلَى الدَّرَّاجَةِ
India is a great country	١٠٧) اَلْهِنْدُ وَطَنٌ عَظِيْمٌ
India is my country	١٠٨) اَلْهِنْدُ وَطَنِي
I love my country	١٠٩) أُحِبُّ وَطَنِي
All Indians are my brothers and sisters	١١٠) اَلْهُنُوْدُ كُلُّهُمْ اِخْوَتِي وَأَخَوَاتِي
Ahmed went to the bank	١١١) ذَهَبَ أَحْمَدُ إِلى الْبَنْكِ
Ayesha is opening the window	١١٢) تَفْتَحُ عَائِشَةُ النَّافِذَةَ
The girl is collecting flowers	١١٣) تَجْمَعُ الْبِنْتُ الأَزْهَارَ
The shoes are made of leather	١١٤) تُصْنَعُ الأَحْذِيَةُ مِنَ الْجِلْدِ
Class room is open	١١٥) حُجْرَةُ الدِّرَاسَةِ مَفْتُوْحَةٌ
The wise man is advising	١١٦) اَلرَّجُلُ العَاقِلُ نَاصِحٌ
The small house is comfortable	١١٧) اَلْبَيْتُ الصَّغِيْرُ مُرِيحٌ
The sitting room is closed	١١٨) غُرْفَةُ الْجُلُوسِ مُغْلَقَةٌ
The red rose is beautiful	١١٩) اَلْوَرْدُ الأَحْمَرُ جَمِيلٌ
The beautiful girl is a singer	١٢٠) اَلْبِنْتُ الجَمِيلَةُ مُغَنِّيَةٌ
Severe cold is painful	١٢١) اَلْبَرْدُ الشَّدِيدُ مُؤْلِمٌ
Useful knowledge is demanded	١٢٢) اَلْعِلْمُ النَّافِعُ مَطْلُوبٌ
Faithful friend is rare	١٢٣) اَلصَّدِيقُ الْوَفِيُّ نَادِرٌ
Independence day is a great day	١٢٤) يَوْمُ الإِسْتِقْلاَلِ يَوْمٌ عَظِيْمٌ

101

The new book is in the library	١٢٥) اَلْكِتَابُ الْجَدِيدُ فِي الْمَكْتَبَةِ
I read an important advertisement	١٢٦) قَرَأْتُ إِعْلاَنًا هَامًّا
The students are playing	١٢٧) اَلطُّلاَّبُ لاَعِبُونَ
The teachers are writing	١٢٨) اَلْمُعَلِّمُونَ كَاتِبُونَ
The schools are open	١٢٩) اَلْمَدَارِسُ مَفْتُوحَةٌ
I am a clerk / I am a writer	١٣٠) أَنَا كَاتِبٌ
He is a manager	١٣١) هُوَ مُدِيرٌ
She is an accountant	١٣٢) هِيَ مُحَاسِبَةٌ
The man is a scholar	١٣٣) اَلرَّجُلُ عَالِمٌ
The boy is tall	١٣٤) اَلْوَلَدُ طَوِيلٌ
You are very tall	١٣٥) أَنْتَ طَوِيلٌ جِدًّا
The nurse is short	١٣٦) اَلْمُمَرِّضَةُ قَصِيرَةٌ
I am very happy today because my son got through the exam in first class	١٣٧) أَنَا مَسْرُورٌ جِدًّا لأَنَّ اِبْنِي نَجَحَ فِي الإِمْتِحَانِ بِالدَّرَجَةِ الأُوْلَى
The chair is comfortable	١٣٨) اَلْكُرْسِيُّ مُرِيحٌ
The boy is intelligent	١٣٩) اَلْوَلَدُ ذَكِيٌّ
This school is good	١٤٠) هَذِهِ الْمَدْرَسَةُ جَيِّدَةٌ
The girl is sitting on the chair	١٤١) اَلْبِنْتُ جَالِسَةٌ عَلَى الكُرْسِيِّ
This bus is coming from New Delhi	١٤٢) هَذِهِ الْحَافِلَةُ قَادِمَةٌ مِن دِلْهِي الجَدِيدَةِ
That bus is going to Agra	١٤٣) تِلْكَ الْحَافِلَةُ ذَاهِبَةٌ إِلَى آغْرَا

Ahmed is returning with Ayesha from the Market	١٤٤) أَحْمَدُ رَاجِعٌ مَعَ عَائِشَةَ مِنَ السُّوقِ
There is a student in the class	١٤٥) فِى الْفَصْلِ طَالِبٌ
There is a newspaper on the table	١٤٦) عَلَى الطَّاوِلَةِ جَرِيدَةٌ
There is a table on the room	١٤٧) فِى الْغُرْفَةِ طَاوِلَةٌ
There is cold water in the fridge	١٤٨) فِى الثَّلاَّجَةِ مَاءٌ بَارِدٌ
On the window there is a curtain	١٤٩) عَلَى النَّافِذَةِ سِتَارَةٌ
His office is far from his house	١٥٠) مَكْتَبُهُ بَعِيدٌ مِن بَيْتِه
She is busy in her office	١٥١) هِيَ مَشْغُولَةٌ فِى مَكْتَبِهَا
My father is sleeping in his room	١٥٢) وَالِدِي نَائِمٌ فِى غُرْفَتِه
Head of the department is sitting in his room	١٥٣) رَئِيسُ الْقِسْمِ جَالِسٌ فِى مَكْتَبِهِ
He is going to his friend's house	١٥٤) هُوَ ذَاهِبٌ إِلَى بَيْتِ صَدِيقِه
The new teacher is a tall man	١٥٥) اَلْمُدَرِّسُ الْجَدِيدُ رَجُلٌ طَوِيلٌ
The little boy is naughty, but intelligent	١٥٦) اَلْوَلَدُ الصَّغِيْرُ شَقِيٌّ، وَلَكِنْ ذَكِيٌّ
The sick man is going to his country	١٥٧) اَلرَّجُلُ الْمَرِيضُ ذَاهِبٌ إِلَى بَلَدِه
He took him to the hospital	١٥٨) أَخَذَهُ إِلَى الْمُسْتَشْفَى
She took her to the nursery	١٥٩) أَخَذَتْهَا إِلَى الرَّوْضَة
They took him to the clinic	١٦٠) أَخَذُوهُ إِلَى الْعِيَادَة

Did he take you to the school?	١٦١) هَلْ أَخَذَكَ اِلَىَ الْمَدْرَسَةِ ؟
My father took me to the market	١٦٢) أَخَذَنِى أَبِى إِلَى السُّوقِ
The girl is smiling	١٦٣) اَلْبِنْتُ بَاسِمَةٌ
The road is narrow	١٦٤) الشَّارِع ضَيِّق
The soldier is brave	١٦٥) اَلْجُنْدِيُّ شُجَاعٌ
The Arabian hospitality is famous	١٦٦) جَوْدُ الْعَرَب مَشْهُورٌ
Character is the foundation of success	١٦٧) اَلْخُلُقُ أَسَاسُ النَّجَاح
Seeking knowledge is obligatory	١٦٨) طَلَبُ الْعِلمِ فَرِيضَةٌ
The doors of the museum are open	١٦٩) أَبْوَابُ الْمَتْحَفِ مَفْتُوْحَةٌ
The lion is the king of the jungle	١٧٠) اَلْأَسَدُ مَلِكُ الْغَابَة
These are two beautiful roses	١٧١) هَاتَانِ وَرْدَتَانِ جَمِيْلَتَانِ
Why have you chosen this language?	١٧٢) لِمَاذَا اخْتَرْتَ هَذِهِ اللُّغَةَ ؟
When do you go to the college?	١٧٣) مَتَى تَذهَبُ إِلَى اَلْكُلِّيَّةِ
Yes indeed, I have seen it several times	١٧٤) بَلَى رَأَيْتُهُ مِرَارًا
Don't you know swimming well?	١٧٥) اَلآ تُجِيدُ السِّبَاحَةُ
I am afraid of swimming	١٧٦) أَخَافُ مِنَ السِّبَاحَةِ

Have you got a watch?	١٧٧) هَلْ عِنْدَكَ سَاعَةٌ؟
Where is the zoo?	١٧٨) اَيْنَ حَدِيقَةُ الْحَيَوَانَاتِ؟
What is result of your exam?	١٧٩) مَا نَتِيجَةُ اِمْتِحَانِكَ؟
What did your teacher say?	١٨٠) مَاذَا قَالَ مُدَرِّسُكَ؟
Which book is with you?	١٨١) أَيُّ كِتَابٍ مَعَكَ؟
Why did you go to Mumbai?	١٨٢) لِمَاذَا ذَهَبْتَ اِلَى مُمْبَاي؟
Why are you traveling?	١٨٣) لِمَاذَا أَنْتَ تُسَافِرُ؟
Who are these tall men?	١٨٤) مَنْ هَؤُلَاءِ الرِّجَالُ الطِّوَالُ؟
Why are you late?	١٨٥) لِمَاذَا أَنْتَ مُتَأَخِّرٌ؟
What happened yesterday?	١٨٦) مَاذَا حَدَثَ اَمْسِ؟
What is the rent of this office?	١٨٧) مَا أُجْرَةُ هَذَا الْمَكْتَبِ؟
My house is near the airport	١٨٨) بَيْتِي قُرْبَ المَطَارِ
He is in the house	١٨٩) هُوَ فِى الْبَيْتِ
She is in the school	١٩٠) هِيَ فِى الْمَدْرَسَةِ
Khalid stayed at home	١٩١) بَقِيَ خَالِدٌ فِى الْبَيْتِ
Where did you go yesterday?	١٩٢) اَيْنَ ذَهَبْتَ الْبَارِحَةَ؟
I went to the beach	١٩٣) ذَهَبْتُ اِلَى الْبَحْرِ
I stayed at home	١٩٤) بَقِيتُ فِى الْبَيْتِ
When did you sleep last night?	١٩٥) مَتَى نِمْتَ الْبَارِحَةَ؟
I slept at nine	١٩٦) نِمْتُ فِى التَّاسِعَةِ

How did you go to Saudi	١٩٧) كَيْفَ ذَهَبْتَ اِلَى السَّعُودِيَّةِ؟
I went by car	١٩٨) ذَهَبْتُ بِالسَّيَّارَةِ
I went by bus	١٩٩) ذَهَبْتُ بِالْبَاصِ/ بِالْحَافِلَةِ
How did you travel?	٢٠٠) كَيْفَ سَافَرْتَ؟
I traveled by plane	٢٠١) سَافَرْتُ بِالطَّائِرَةِ
When did you reach Jeddah?	٢٠٢) مَتَى وَصَلْتَ جِدَّةَ؟
I reached at one o' clock	٢٠٣) وَصَلْتُ فِى الْوَاحِدَةِ
Is he at home?	٢٠٤) هَلْ هُوَ فِى الْبَيْتِ؟
Have you been to Egypt?	٢٠٥) هَلْ ذَهَبْتَ اِلَى مِصْرَ؟
Are you sure?	٢٠٦) هَلْ اَنْتَ مُتَأَكِّدٌ؟
What do you think, Ahmed?	٢٠٧) مَا رَأْيُكَ يَا أَحْمَدُ؟
They went to India last week	٢٠٨) سَافَرُوا اِلَى الْهِنْدِ فِي الْأُسْبُوعِ الْمَاضِي
He spoke to us on the phone	٢٠٩) كَلَّمَنَا عَلَى التِّلِفُونِ
She spoke to me this morning	٢١٠) كَلَّمَتْنِي هَذَا الصَّبَاحَ
They fed us well	٢١١) أَطْعَمُونَا جَيِّدًا
I like the Arabic language	٢١٢) أُحِبُّ اللُّغَةَ الْعَرَبِيَّةَ
This is a suitable subject	٢١٣) هَذَا مَوْضُوعٌ مُنَاسِبٌ
I would like to go to the beach	٢١٤) أُحِبُّ أَنْ اَذْهَبَ اِلَى الْبَحْرِ
Do you like your work?	٢١٥) هَلْ تُحِبُّ عَمَلَكَ؟
I am a teacher at Ideal Indian School.	٢١٦) أَنَا مُدَرِّسٌ فِى الْمَدْرَسَةِ الْهِنْدِيَّةِ الْمِثَالِيَّةِ

Does Monday suit you?	٢١٧) هَلْ يُنَاسِبُكَ الاثْنَيْنِ؟
Yes, it suits me	٢١٨) نَعَمْ يُنَاسِبُنِى
I go to work every morning	٢١٩) أَذْهَبُ إِلَى الْعَمَلِ كُلَّ صَبَاح
I will go to work day after tomorrow	٢٢٠) سَأَذْهَبُ إِلَى الْعَمَلِ بَعْدَ غَدٍ
I will stay in Doha till June	٢٢١) سَأَبْقَى فِى الدَّوْحَةِ حَتَّى يُونْيُو
I won't come back until next Sunday	٢٢٢) لَنْ اَرْجِعَ حَتَّى الاَحَدَ الْمُسْتَقْبِلِ
When will you come back?	٢٢٣) مَتَى سَتَعُودُ؟
God willing, I will come back this Saturday	٢٢٤) سَأَرْجِعُ اِنْ شَاءَ اللهُ هَذَا السَّبْتِ
Have you read this book?	٢٢٥) هَلْ قَرَأْتَ هَذَا الْكِتَابَ؟
Do you like to go to the beach?	٢٢٦) هَلْ تُحِبُّ اَنْ تَذْهَبَ اِلَى الْبَحْرِ؟
Why isn't Ahmed playing with you	٢٢٧) لِمَاذَا لاَيَلْعَبُ أَحْمَدُ مَعَكُمْ؟
We called him, but he did not answer	٢٢٨) نَادَيْنَاهُ لَكِنَّهُ لَمْ يَرُدَّ
The weather was nice	٢٢٩) كَانَ الطَّقْسُ جَمِيلاً
Do we come back before four o' clock	٢٣٠) هَلْ نَرْجِعُ قَبْلَ الرَّابِعَةِ؟
Do you want to go for shopping with me?	٢٣١) هَلْ تُرِيدُ أَنْ تَأْتِيَ مَعِى اِلَى السُّوقِ؟
This shop has everything	٢٣٢) هَذَا الْمَحَلُّ عِنْدَهُ كُلُّ شَيْئٍ
I need some papers	٢٣٣) أَحْتَاجُ بَعْضَ الأَوْرَاقِ
He needs some money	٢٣٤) يَحْتَاجُ بَعْضَ الْمَالِ

107

She needs some time	٢٣٥) تَحْتَاجُ بَعْضَ الْوَقْتِ
Will you go with us to the cinema?	٢٣٦) هَلْ سَتَذْهَبُ مَعَنَا إِلَى السِّيْنِمَا؟
Has the plane arrived or will it be late?	٢٣٧) هَلْ وَصَلَتِ الطَّائِرَةُ اَمْ سَتَتَأَخَّرُ؟
Did you like this shirt?	٢٣٨) هَلْ أَعْجَبَكَ هَذَا الْقَمِيصُ؟
Would you direct me to the Principal's office?	٢٣٩) هَلْ تَدُلُّنِى عَلَى مَكْتَبِ الْمُدِيرِ؟
I did not like this colour	٢٤٠) لَمْ يُعْجِبْنِى هَذَا اللَّوْنُ
I did not like its smell	٢٤١) لَمْ تُعْجِبْنِى رَائِحَتَهُ
Why don't you eat with us today?	٢٤٢) لِمَاذَا لاَتَأْكُلُ مَعَنَا الْيَوْمَ؟
Shall we go to the club today?	٢٤٣) هَلْ نَذْهَبُ النَّادِي الْيَوْمَ؟
Why don't you invite Ahmed to dinner today?	٢٤٤) لِمَاذَا لاَ تَدْعُو أَحْمَدَ إِلَى عَشَاءٍ الْيَوْمَ؟
Ahmed doesn't like Indian food	٢٤٥) أَحْمَدُ لاَ يُحِبُّ الأَكْلَ الْهِنْدِيَّ
Didn't you like the lesson?	٢٤٦) اَلَمْ يُعْجِبْكَ الدَّرْسُ؟
My mother cooks every day	٢٤٧) تَطْبُخُ أُمِّى كُلَّ يَوْمٍ
India is an agricultural country	٢٤٨) اَلْهِنْدُ بَلَدٌ زِرَاعِيٌّ
I want to be an engineer	٢٤٩) أُرِيدُ أَنْ أَكُونَ مُهَنْدِسًا
She wants to be a doctor	٢٥٠) تُرِيدُ أَنْ تَكُونَ طَبِيَبَةً
He wants to be an accountant	٢٥١) يُرِيدُ أَنْ يَكُونَ مُحَاسِبًا
My brother wants to be a pilot	٢٥٢) يُرِيدُ أَخِى أَنْ يَكُونَ طَيَّارًا

This lesson is easy	٢٥٣) هَذَا الدَّرْسُ سَهْلٌ
Her son is an industrious student	٢٥٤) ابْنُهَا طَالِبٌ مُجْتَهِدٌ
You (a girl) don't enter his room	٢٥٥) لاَ تَدْخُلِي غُرْفَتَهُ
You (F.plural) don't play in the class	٢٥٦) لاَ تَلْعَبْنَ فِى الْفَصْلِ
They (M.plural) went out of the class and went to the principal	٢٥٧) خَرَجُوا مِنَ الْفَصْلِ وَ ذَهَبُوا إِلَى الْمُدِيرِ
How many new students are there in your class?	٢٥٨) كَمْ طَالِبًا جَدِيدًا فِى فَصْلِكُمْ؟
How many students (girls) are there in your school?	٢٥٩) كَم طَالِبَةً فِى مَدْرَسَتِكُنَّ
The new principal is very tall.	٢٦٠) اَلْمُدِيرُ الْجَدِيدُ طَوِيلٌ جِدًّا
The boys are playing football	٢٦١) يَلْعَبُ الأَوْلاَدُ كُرَةَ الْقَدَمِ
The girl plucked a flower	٢٦٢) قَطَفَتِ الْبِنْتُ زَهْرَةً
The monkey snatched the scarf of the girl	٢٦٣) خَطَفَ الْقِرْدُ رِدَاءَ الْبِنْتِ
Our teacher is good man	٢٦٤) مُدَرِّسُنَا رَجُلٌ صَالِحٌ
We, in India prefer tea with milk	٢٦٥) نَحْنُ فِى الْهِنْدِ نُفَضِّلُ الشَّايَ بِالْحَلِيبِ
Arabs prefer tea without milk	٢٦٦) يُفَضِّلُ الْعَرَبُ الشَّايَ بِدُونِ حَلِيبٍ
Righteous caliphs are four	٢٦٧) اَلْخُلَفَاءُ الرَّاشِدُونَ أَرْبَعَةٌ
Prophet (PBUH) was born in Makka	٢٦٨) وُلِدَ النَّبِيُّ صَلَّى اللهُ عَلَيْهِ وَسَلَّمَ بِمَكَّةَ

٢٦٩) كَانَ جَدِّى مُدِيرَ شَرِكَةٍ عَالَمِيَّةٍ	My grandfather was a manager of an international company
٢٧٠) قَدْ كَتَبَ الْمُدَرِّسُ الْأَجْوِبَةَ عَلَى السَّبُّورَةِ	The teacher has written the answers on the blackboard
٢٧١) مَا فَتَحَ الْفَرَّاشُ بَابَ الْفَصْلِ	The peon did not open the door of the class
٢٧٢) أَخَذَتِ الْبِنْتُ الصَّغِيرَةُ التُّفَّاحَةَ مِنَ الثَّلَّاجَةِ	The little girl took an apple from the fridge
٢٧٣) جَلَسَتِ الْبِنْتُ فِى الْمَكْتَبَةِ وَ قَرَأَتِ الْجَرَائِدَ الْمَحَلِّيَّةَ	The girl sat in the library and read local newspapers
٢٧٤) ذَهَبَتْ إِلَى بَيْتِ مُدَرِّسِهَا صَبَاحًا	She went to the house of her teacher in the morning
٢٧٥) تَجْلِسُ خَدِيجَةُ عَلَى الْكُرْسِيِّ وَ تُرَاجِعُ الدُّرُوسَ الْقَدِيمَةَ	Khadija sits on the chair and revises the old lessons
٢٧٦) هَلْ تَسْكُنُ فِى ذَلِكَ الْبَيْتِ الْكَبِيرِ؟	Does she live in that big house?
٢٧٧) هَلْ تَقْرَأُ وَ تَكْتُبُ الْعَرَبِيَّةَ فِى مَدْرَسَتِكَ؟	Do you read and write Arabic in your school?
٢٧٨) لَا يَسْكُنُ خَالِدٌ فِى هَذِهِ الْمَدِينَةِ	Khalid does not live in this city
٢٧٩) اِذْهَبْ إِلَى غُرْفَتِكَ وَاسْتَرِحْ	Go to your room and relax
٢٨٠) اِفْتَحْ دَفْتَرَكَ وَاكْتُبْ مَقَالَةً قَصِيرَةً عَنْ مَدْرَسَتِكَ	Open your note book and write a short essay about your school.

Khadija, go to school every day early	٢٨١) يَا خَدِيجَةُ اذْهَبِي إِلَى الْمَدْرَسَةِ كُلَّ يَوْمٍ مُبَكِّرَةً
Write (to a girl) your name on the new book	٢٨٢) اُكْتُبِي اسْمَكِ عَلَى الْكِتَابِ الْجَدِيدِ
Don't open the door now	٢٨٣) لَا تَفْتَحْ الْبَابَ الآنَ
Don't play in the street/ road	٢٨٤) لَا تَلْعَبِي فِى الشَّارِعِ
Is he coming now?	٢٨٥) هَلْ هُوَ قَادِمٌ الآنَ
Are you happy now?	٢٨٦) هَلْ أَنْتَ سَعِيدٌ الآنَ؟
Am I late today?	٢٨٧) هَل أَنَا مُتَأَخِّرٌ الَيَوْمَ؟
Did you attend the meeting yesterday?	٢٨٨) هَلْ حَضَرْتَ الإجْتِمَاعَ أَمْسِ؟
Do you study English every day?	٢٨٩) هَلْ تَدْرُسُ الإنْجلِيزِيَّة كُلَّ يَوْمٍ؟
Will you write a story about you in Arabic?	٢٩٠) هَلْ تَكْتُبُ قِصَّةً عَنْكَ فِى الْعَرَبِيَّةِ؟
When will you visit me?	٢٩١) مَتَى سَتَزُورُنِى؟
When does your brother return from his office?	٢٩٢) مَتَى يَعُودُ أَخُوكَ مِن مَكْتَبِهِ؟
Her brother won the first prize in the competition	٢٩٣) فَازَ أَخُوهَا فِى الْجَائِزَةِ الأُولَى فِى الْمُسَابَقَةِ
The aeroplane flies in the sky	٢٩٤) تَطِيرُ الطَّائِرَةُ فِى السَّمَاءِ
The child fell on the ground and cried	٢٩٥) سَقَطَ الطِّفْلُ عَلَى الأَرْضِ فَبَكَى

111

٢٩٦) أَيْنَ يَقَعُ مَكْتَبُكَ؟ — Where is your office situated?

٢٩٧) يَقَعُ مَكْتَبِي فِي الْمَدِينَةِ الْجَدِيدَةِ — My office is situated in the new city

٢٩٨) سَوْفَ أَزُورُهُ فِى دِلْهِى الْعَام الْقَادِم / السَّنَة الْقَادِمَة — I will visit him in Delhi next year

٢٩٩) سَيَرْجِعُ مِنْ مَكْتَبِهِ مَسَاءًا — He will return from his office in the evening

٣٠٠) سَتَعُودُ أُخْتُهُ مِنْ لَنْدَن اَلشَّهْرَ الْقَادِمَ — His sister will return from London next month

٣٠١) هَلْ تَسْمَعُ الأَخْبَارَ الإِنْجِلِيزِيَّةَ صَبَاحًا؟ — Do you listen to English news in the morning

٣٠٢) أَقْرَأُ الْجَرِيدَةَ الْعَرَبِيَّةَ صَبَاحًا — I read the Arabic newspaper in the morning

٣٠٣) يَسْكُنُ الْمُدِيرُ خَلْفَ هَذَا الْبَيْتِ — The principal lives behind this house

٣٠٤) أَمَامَ الْمَدْرَسَةِ مَطْعَمٌ — There is a restaurant in front of the school.

٣٠٥) تَرَكَ الْمُدَرِّسُ حَقِيبَتَهُ تَحْتَ الطَّاوِلَةِ — The teacher left his bag under the table

٣٠٦) خَلْفَ الْمَدْرَسَةِ مَلْعَبٌ كَبِيرٌ — There is a big playground behind the school.

٣٠٧) بِجِوَارِ الْبَابِ نَافِذَةٌ صَغِيرَةٌ — There is a small window by the side of the door

112

The train passed by the main market   ٣٠٨) مَرَّ الْقِطَارُ بِالسُّوقِ الرَّئِيسِيّ

The thief ran away in the darkness   ٣٠٩) فَرَّ السَّارِقُ فِى الظَّلَام

Your two daughters are playing in the park (garden)   ٣١٠) بِنْتَاكُمَا لَاعِبَتَانِ فِى الْحَدِيقَة

I met two brothers of Khadija in the exhibition   ٣١١) لَقَيْتُ أَخَوَي خَدِيجَةَ فِى الْمَعْرِض

Two officials of the Indian embassy are absent today   ٣١٢) مُوَظَّفَا السِّفَارَةِ الْهِنْدِيَّةِ غَائِبَانِ الْيَوْمَ

Two daughters of Majid study in two different schools   ٣١٣) تَدْرُسُ بِنْتَا مَاجِدٍ فِى مَدْرَسَتَيْنِ مُخْتَلِفَيْن

The birds live in their nests   ٣١٤) تَعِيشُ الطُّيُورُ فِى عُشَاشِهَا

The girls went to their houses   ٣١٥) ذَهَبَتِ الْبَنَاتُ اِلَى بُيُوتِهِنَّ

The government offices in the Arabian gulf are closed on Friday   ٣١٦) اَلْمَكَاتِبُ الْحُكُومِيَّةُ فِى الْخَلِيجِ الْعَرَبِ مُغْلَقَةٌ يَوْمَ الْجُمُعَة

These men work in that small factory   ٣١٧) يَعْمَلُ هَؤُلَاءِ الرِّجَالُ فِى ذَالِك الْمَصْنَعِ الصَّغِير

These engineers are very hard working   ٣١٨) هَؤُلَاءِ الْمُهَنْدِسُوْنَ مُجْتَهِدُونَ جِدًّا

I bought many English magazines today   ٣١٩) اِشْتَرَيْتُ الْمَجَلَّاتِ الإِنْجِلِيزِيَّةَ كَثِيرَةَ الْيَوْمَ

The gate of the school is opened every morning   ٣٢٠) يُفْتَحُ بَابُ الْمَدْرَسَةِ كُلَّ صَبَاح

٣٢١) بِيعَ هَذَا الْمَحَلُّ فِى الأُسْبُوع الْمَاضِى   This shop was sold last week

٣٢٢) لاَ يُفْتَحُ ذَلِكَ الْمَكْتَبُ كُلَّ يَوْمٍ   That office is not opened every day

٣٢٣) مَتَى تَبْدَأُ الْعُطْلَةُ الصَّيْفِيَّةُ؟   When does the summer vacation begin?

٣٢٤) اَلْفَلاَّحُ سَعِيدٌ بِزَرْع الأَرُزِّ   The farmer is happy with the cultivation of rice

٣٢٥) يَعْمَلُ الْفَلاَّحُ فِى الْحَقْل   The farmer works in the field

٣٢٦) هَذِه الأُسْرَةُ تَشْغَلُ مِنَ الصَّبَاح اِلى الْغُرُوبِ   This family works from morning till sunset

٣٢٧) اَلْيَدُ الْعُلْيَا خَيْرٌ مِنَ الْيَدِ السُّفْلَى   The upper hand (giving hand) is better than the lower hand (receiving hand)

٣٢٨) اَلْعِلْمُ خَيْرٌ مِنَ الثَّرْوَةِ   Knowledge is better than wealth

٣٢٩) اَلإتِّحَادُ قُوَّةٌ   Unity is strength

٣٣٠) الوِقَايَةُ خَيْرٌ مِنَ الْمُعَالَجَة   Prevention is better than cure

٣٣١) اَلْوَقْتُ مَالٌ   Time is money

٣٣٢) مَنْ حَفَرَ حُفْرَةً يَقَعُ فِيهَا   One who digs a ditch falls in it

٣٣٣) لَقِيْتُهَا فِىْ الْمَكْتَبَة الْيَوْمَ   I met her in the library today

٣٣٤) لَقَيْتُهُ فِى النَّادِي أَمْسِ   I met him in the club yesterday

٣٣٥) هَلْ لَدَيْكَ حِسَابٌ فِى الْمَصْرَفِ   Have you got an account in the bank?

٣٣٦) عَلَيَّ أَنْ أَذْهَبَ اِلَى الْمَصْنَع الْيَوْمَ   I must go to the factory today

John wants to learn Arabic.	٣٣٧) يُرِيدُ جُونُ أَنْ يَتَعَلَّمَ الْعَرَبِيَّةَ
I spoke to her on phone today	٣٣٨) كَلَّمْتُهَا الْيَوْمَ عَلَى الْهَاتِفِ
What are you doing now?	٣٣٩) مَاذَا تَفْعَلُ الْآنَ؟
Is this her address?	٣٤٠) أَهَذَا عُنْوَانُهَا؟
Where did you write his address?	٣٤١) أَيْنَ كَتَبْتَ عُنْوَانَهُ؟
When was this school built?	٣٤٢) مَتَى بُنِيَتْ هَذِهِ الْمَدْرَسَةُ؟
Why did you do that?	٣٤٣) لِمَاذَا فَعَلْتَ ذَلِكَ؟
What is the exchange rate of American dollar today?	٣٤٤) كَمْ سِعْرُ الدُّولَارِ الأَمْرِيكِي الْيَوْمَ؟
What did you do in Doha?	٣٤٥) مَاذَا فَعَلْتَ فِي الدَّوْحَةِ؟
I have never worked in this company	٣٤٦) مَا عَمِلْتُ أَبَدًا فِي هَذِهِ الشَّرِكَةِ؟
I wasn't at home	٣٤٧) لَمْ أَكُنْ فِي الْبَيْتِ
I will not travel this year	٣٤٨) لَنْ أُسَافِرَ هَذَا الْعَامَ
I don't have children	٣٤٩) لَيْسَ لَدَيَّ أَوْلَادٌ
This law is unjust	٣٥٠) هَذَا الْقَانُونُ غَيْرُ عَادِلٍ
Do you promise to write to me every week	٣٥١) هَلْ تَعِدُنِي بِأَنْ تَكْتُبَ لِي كُلَّ أُسْبُوعٍ
I haven't spoken to him for a year	٣٥٢) مَا كَلَّمْتُهُ مُنْذُ سَنَةٍ
The sparrow is in the tree	٣٥٣) الْعُصْفُورُ عَلَى الشَّجَرَةِ
The minister returned to the capital	٣٥٤) عَادَ الْوَزِيرُ إِلَى الْعَاصِمَةِ
Don't play with fire	٣٥٥) لَا تَلْعَبْ بِالنَّارِ
The reward is for the winner	٣٥٦) الْجَائِزَةُ لِلسَّابِقِ

He is fond of reading	٣٥٧) هُوَ مُولَعٌ بِالْقِرَاءَةِ
The minister has left Delhi	٣٥٨) قَدْ غَادَرَ الْوَزِيرُ دِلْهِي
I invited my friends to a tea party	٣٥٩) دَعَوْتُ أَصْدِقَائِي لِحَفْلَةِ الشَّايِ
I listened the advice of my teacher	٣٦٠) سَمِعْتُ نَصِيْحَةَ مُدَرِّسِي
The student opened his book	٣٦١) فَتَحَ الطَّالِبُ كِتَابَهُ
The principal has returned from India	٣٦٢) قَدْ عَادَ الْمُدِيرُ مِنَ الْهِنْدِ
My brother witnessed the football match yesterday	٣٦٣) شَاهَدَ أَخِي مُبَارَاةَ كُرَةِ الْقَدَمِ أَمْسِ
Heat becomes severe in summer	٣٦٤) يَشْتَدُّ الْحَرُّ فِى الصَّيْفِ
The child is crying in the cradle	٣٦٥) يَبْكِي الطِّفْلُ فِى الْمَهْدِ
One who makes haste will repent	٣٦٦) مَنْ يَسْتَعْجِلْ يَنْدَمْ
The girl is cleaning the cloth	٣٦٧) تَنْظِفُ الْبِنْتُ الثِّيَابَ
Don't put off today's work for tomorrow	٣٦٨) لَا تُؤَخِّرْ عَمَلَ الْيَوْمِ إِلَى غَدٍ
Go to sleep early and get up early	٣٦٩) نَمْ مُبَكِّرًا وَ قُمْ مُبَكِّرًا
The money has been stolen	٣٧٠) قَدْ سُرِقَ الْمَالُ
Public gardens are being developed	٣٧١) تَنْشَأُ الْحَدَائِقُ الْعَامَّةُ
The lazy person will never succeed	٣٧٢) لَنْ يَنْجَحَ الْكَسْلَانُ
Be polite, so that you could be loved	٣٧٣) كُنْ مُؤَدِّبًا كَيْ تَكُونَ مَحْبُوبًا
Don't grieve, certainly Allah is with us	٣٧٤) لَا تَحْزَنْ إِنَّ اللهَ مَعَنَا
The patient is still in the hospital	٣٧٥) مَا زَالَ الْمَرِيضُ فِي الْمُسْتَشْفَى
Perhaps the train is reaching the station as per the schedule	٣٧٦) لَعَلَّ الْقِطَارَ يَصِلُ الْمَحَطَّةَ فِى مَوْعِدِهِ

The tree is big , but it is without fruit	٣٧٧) اَلشَّجَرَةُ كَبِيرَةٌ لَكِنَّهَا غَيْرُ مُثْمِرَةٍ
It pleases me to participate in this discussion	٣٧٨) يَسُرُّنِي أَنْ أَشْتَرِكَ فِى هَذِهِ الْمُنَاقَشَةِ
Perhaps the culprit is free	٣٧٩) لَعَلَّ الْمُجْرِمَ طَلِيقٌ
Perhaps the goal is near	٣٨٠) لَعَلَّ الْهَدَفَ قَرِيبٌ
No jealous person is comfortable	٣٨١) لاَ حَاسِدٌ مُسْتَرِيحًا
None who consults in his affairs is repentant	٣٨٢) لاَ مُسْتَشِيرٍ فِى أُمُورِه نَادِمًا
Certainly Taj Mahal is beautiful	٣٨٣) اِنَّ تَاج مَحَل جَمِيلٌ
Certainly summer is not far off	٣٨٤) اِنَّ الصَّيْفَ غَيْرُ بَعِيدٍ
Knowledge is more useful than wealth	٣٨٥) اَلْعِلْمُ اَنْفَعُ مِنَ الْمَالِ
The aeroplane is faster than the train	٣٨٦) اَلطَّيَّارَةُ اَسْرَعُ مِنَ الْقِطَارِ
A stranger is the relative of other stranger	٣٨٧) كُلُّ غَرِيبٍ لِلْغَرِيبِ نَسِيبٌ
Charity begins at home	٣٨٨) اَلاَقْرَبُوْنَ أَوْلَى بِالْمَعْرُوفِ
Man proposes and God disposes	٣٨٩) اَلإِنْسَانُ بِالتَّفْكِيرِ وَاللهُ بِالتَّدبِيرِ
One who sows will reap	٣٩٠) مَنْ زَرَعَ حَصَدَ
Strike the iron when it is hot	٣٩١) اِضْرِبْ الْحَدِيدَ حَامِيًا
As you sow, so shall you reap	٣٩٢) كَمَا تَزْرَعُ تَحْصُدُ
A friend in need is a friend indeed	٣٩٣) اَلصَّدِيقُ عِنْدَ الضِّيقِ
If speech is silver, silence is gold	٣٩٤) اِذَا كَانَ الْكَلاَمُ مِنْ فِضَّةٍ فَالسُّكُوتُ مِنَ ذَهَبٍ

Little knowledge is dangerous	اَلْعِلْمُ الْقَلِيلُ خَطِرٌ	٣٩٥)
Opportunities do not wait	اَلْفُرَصُ لاَتَنْتَظِرُ	٣٩٦)
Laziness is the key to poverty	اَلْكَسْلُ مِفْتَاحُ الْفَقْرِ	٣٩٧)
Necessity is the mother of inventions	اَلْحَاجَةُ أُمُّ الإِخْتِرَاعِ	٣٩٨)
All that glitters is not gold	لَيْسَ كُلَّمَا يَلْمَعُ ذَهَباً	٣٩٩)
Too many cooks spoil the soup	كَثْرَةُ الطَّبَّاخِينَ تُفْسِدُ الطَّبْخَةَ	٤٠٠)
Empty vessel makes much noise	اَلإِنَاءُ الْفَارِغُ يَرِنُّ كَثِيراً	٤٠١)
Actions speak more than words	اَلأَعْمَالُ أَبْلَغُ مِنَ الأَقْوَالِ	٤٠٢)
Send this draft by speed post	أَرْسِلْ هَذِهِ الْحَوَالَةَ بِالْبَرِيدِ الْعَاجِلِ	٤٠٣)
Saving is better than spending	اَلاِتِّخَاذُ خَيْرٌ مِنَ الاِنْفَاقِ	٤٠٤)
Banking sector is very strong in our country	قِطَاعُ الْمَصَارِفِ قَوِيٌّ جِدًّا فِى بَلَدِنَا	٤٠٥)
Euro is the most popular currency in the world	يُورُوْ عُمْلَةٌ وَاسِعَةُ التَّرْوِيجِ فِى الْعَالَمِ	٤٠٦)
Value of rupee has fallen considerably	قَدِ انْخَفَضَتْ قِيمَةُ الرُّوبِيَّةِ بِدَرَجَةٍ كَبِيرَةٍ	٤٠٧)
Do you have change for 100 dollars?	هَلْ عِنْدَكَ صَرْفٌ لِمِائَةِ دُوْلاَرٍ؟	٤٠٨)
The engineer drew parallel lines	رَسَمَ الْمُهَنْدِسُ خُطُوطًا مُوَازِيَةً	٤٠٩)
Numbers are divided into odd and even numbers	تَنْقَسِمُ الأَعْدَادُ إِلَى فَرْدٍ وَ زَوْجٍ	٤١٠)
You (two) are teachers in the school.	أَنْتُمَا مُدَرِّسَانِ فِىْ الْمَدْرَسَةِ	١ ٠٠
They (two) live in Old Delhi	هُمَا يَسْكُنَانِ فِى دِلْهِي الْقَدِيمَةِ	٤١٢)

My brother works in the factory	٤١٣) أَخِيْ يَعْمَلُ فِى الْمَصْنَعِ
Who traveled to Agra?	٤١٤) مَنْ سَافَرَ إِلَى آغْرَا؟
Arabic language is very beautiful	٤١٥) اَللُّغَةُ الْعَرَبِيَّةُ جَمِيْلَةٌ جِدًّا
What is the price of this pen?	٤١٦) بِكَمْ اشْتَرَيْتَ هَذَا الْقَلَمَ؟
Its price is Rs.5	٤١٧) ثَمَنُهُ خَمْسُ رُوْبِيَّاتٍ
We will never go to that park	٤١٨) لَنْ نَذْهَبَ إِلَى تِلْكَ الْحَدِيْقَةِ
Did you read this book?	٤١٩) هَلْ قَرَأْتَ هَذَا الْكِتَابَ؟
It is a book of Indian history	٤٢٠) ذَلِكَ كِتَابُ تَارِيْخِ الْهِنْدِ
It is prescribed in our course	٤٢١) ذَلِكَ مُعَيَّنٌ فِى مَنْهَجِنَا
The railway station is near our college	٤٢٢) مَحَطَّةُ الْقِطَارِ قَرِيْبَةٌ مِنْ كُلِّيَّتِنَا
Have you travelled by train?	٤٢٣) هَلْ سَافَرْتَ بِالْقِطَارِ؟
When our friend came, we received him	٤٢٤) حِيْنَمَا قَدَمَ صَدِيْقُنَا اسْتَقْبَلْنَاهُ
They play football every day	٤٢٥) يَلْعَبُوْنَ كُرَةَ الْقَدَمِ كُلَّ يَوْمٍ
Our college is the best	٤٢٦) كُلِّيَّتُنَا أَحْسَنُ
My teacher is very sincere	٤٢٧) مُدَرِّسِى مُخْلِصٌ جِدًّا
The library of the school is open now	٤٢٨) مَكْتَبَةُ الْمَدْرَسَةِ مَفْتُوْحَةٌ اَلْآنَ
Do you (men) want to travel?	٤٢٩) هَلْ تُرِيْدُوْنَ أَنْ تُسَافِرُوا؟
Their brother lives in Delhi	٤٣٠) يَسْكُنُ أَخُوْهُمْ فِى دِلْهِي
The town is far away	٤٣١) اَلْمَدِيْنَةُ بَعِيْدَةٌ جِدًّا

٤٣٢) أَقْلَامُ خَالِدٍ عَلَى الطَّاوِلَةِ — The pens of Khalid are on the table

٤٣٣) عَلَى الطَّاوِلَةِ أَحَدَ عَشَرَ كِتَابًا — There are 11 pens on the table

٤٣٤) أَنَا مُدَرِّسُ اللُّغَةِ الْعَرَبِيَّةِ — I am a teacher of Arabic

٤٣٥) سَيَّارَتِى خَارِجَ الْمَطَارِ — My car is outside the airport

٤٣٦) أَنَا الآنُ فِى صَالَةِ الاِنْتِظَارِ — Now I am in the waiting room

٤٣٧) أَنَا فِى انْتِظَارِ صَدِيقِي وَ أُسْرَتِهِ — I am waiting for my friend and his family

٤٣٨) صَدِيقِى هِنْدِيّ هُوَ رَجُلُ أَعْمَالٍ كَبِيرٌ — My friend is an Indian. He is a big business man

٤٣٩) هَلْ أَنْتَ رَجُلُ أَعْمَالٍ؟ — Are you a business man?

٤٤٠) عِنْدَنَا بُسْتَانِيٌّ يَعْمَلُ فِى الْحَدِيقَةِ — We have a gardener who works in the garden

٤٤١) هَلْ تَذْهَبُ إِلَى مَكْتَبِكَ بِالسَّيَّارَةِ؟ — Do you go to your office by car?

٤٤٢) هَلْ نَذْهَبُ إِلَى الْحَدِيقَةِ الْيَوْمَ؟ — Shall we go to the park today?

٤٤٣) هَلْ تَسْكُنُ مَعَ أُسْرَتِكَ / عَائِلَتِكَ؟ — Do you live with your family?

٤٤٤) لاَ، أَسْكُنُ مَعَ صَدِيْقٍ — No I live with a friend

٤٤٥) هَل الشُّقَّةُ بَعِيْدَةٌ عَنِ الْجَامِعَةِ؟ — Is the flat far away from the university?

٤٤٦) لاَ، هِيَ قَرِيبَةٌ مِنَ الْجَامِعَةِ — No, It is near the university

٤٤٧) مَاذَا تَشْرَبُ بَعْدَ الأَكْلِ يَا اِسْمَاعِيلُ؟ — What would you like to drink after the meal, Ismail?

What do we do today?	٤٤٨) مَاذَا نَفْعَلُ الْيَوْمَ؟
I have got a new idea	٤٤٩) عِنْدِي فِكْرَةٌ جَدِيدَةٌ
Do you like to ride a camel?	٤٥٠) هَلْ تُحِبُّ أَنْ تَرْكَبَ الْجَمَلَ؟
Are you a student in the university?	٤٥١) هَلْ أَنْتَ طَالِبٌ فِى الْجَامِعَةِ؟
Yesterday I went to hire a car	٤٥٢) أَمْسِ ذَهَبْتُ لِاسْتِئْجَارِ سَيَّارَةٍ
I want to hire a car for a week	٤٥٣) أُرِيدُ اسْتِئْجَارَ سَيَّارَةٍ لِمُدَّةِ أُسْبُوعٍ
Have you got a driving licence?	٤٥٤) هَلْ عِنْدَكَ رُخْصَةُ قِيَادَةٍ؟
Yes, I have an international licence	٤٥٥) نَعَمْ عِنْدِى رُخْصَةٌ دُوَلِيَّةٌ
Have you visited Cairo?	٤٥٦) هَلْ زُرْتَ الْقَاهِرَةَ؟
What can I do for you?	٤٥٧) أَيَّ خِدْمَةٍ؟
Can I help you?	٤٥٨) مُمْكِن أُسَاعِدُكَ
I would like to cash this cheque	٤٥٩) أُرِيدُ صَرْفَ هَذَا الشِّيكِ
Have you got an account in the bank?	٤٦٠) هَلْ لَكَ حِسَابٌ فِى الْبَنْكِ؟
Are you an employee in this bank?	٤٦١) هَلْ أَنْتَ مُوَظَّفٌ فِى هَذَا الْبَنْكِ؟
I want to buy a piece of cloth	٤٦٢) أُرِيدُ شِرَاءَ قِطْعَةِ قُمَاشٍ
Did your sister go with you?	٤٦٣) هَلْ ذَهَبَتْ أُخْتُكَ مَعَكَ؟
I was in the market	٤٦٤) كُنْتُ فِى السُّوقِ

121

٤٦٥) مَاذَا اشْتَرَيْتَ مِنَ السُّوقِ؟ — What did you buy from the market?

٤٦٦) مَاذَا تُرِيدُ أَنْ تَشْتَرِيَ؟ — What do you want to buy?

٤٦٧) هَلْ أَكَلْتَ لَحْمَ الْجَمَلِ؟ — Have you ever eaten camel meat?

٤٦٨) اَلطَّبِيبُ مَشْغُولٌ دَائِمًا — The doctor is always busy

٤٦٩) أُرِيدُ أَنْ أَشْتَرِيَ فُسْتَانًا — I want to buy a dress

٤٧٠) هَلْ يُعْجِبُكَ هَذَا الْفُسْتَانُ؟ — Do you like this dress?

٤٧١) مَاذَا أَكَلْتَ أَمْسِ؟ — What did you eat yesterday?

٤٧٢) هَلْ ذَهَبْتَ اِلَى الطَّبِيبِ؟ — Did you go to the doctor?

٤٧٣) هَلْ فَحَصَكَ؟ — Did he examine you?

٤٧٤) مَا هِيَ الْمَشَاكِلُ الرَّئِيسِيَّةُ فِى مُجْتَمَعِنَا؟ — What are the main problems in our society?

٤٧٥) كَيْفَ نُعَالِجُ هَذِهِ الْمَشَاكِلَ؟ — How do we treat these problems?

٤٧٦) أَيْنَ تَذْهَبُ هَذِهِ اللَّيْلَةَ؟ — Where are you going tonight?

٤٧٧) أُرِيدُ أَنْ أَذْهَبَ اِلَى النَّادِي — I want to go to the club

٤٧٨) لِمَاذَا تُرِيدُ أَنْ تَذْهَبَ اِلَى النَّادِي؟ — Why do you want to go to the club?

٤٧٩) أُرِيدُ أَنْ أُقَابِلَ بَعْضَ أَصْدِقَائِي — I want to meet some of my friends

٤٨٠) هَلْ قَرَأْتُمْ جَرَائِدَ الصَّبَاح يَا أَوْلَادُ؟ — Have you read the morning newspaper?

٤٨١) هَلْ أَنْتَ سَعِيدٌ مَعَ زَوْجَتِكَ؟ — Are you happy with your wife?

Where do you go for your summer holidays?	٤٨٢) أَيْنَ تَذْهَبُ لِتَقْضِيَ عُطْلَتَكَ الصَّيْفِيَّة؟
Did you watch the football match yesterday?	٤٨٣) هَلْ شَاهَدْتَ مُبَارَاةَ كُرَةِ الْقَدَمِ أَمْسٍ؟
I read an important advertisement in the newspaper today	٤٨٤) قَرَأْتُ اعْلاَنًا مُهِمًّا فِى الْجَرِيدَةِ الْيَوْم
What are you going to do next year?	٤٨٥) مَاذَا سَتَعْمَلُ فِى الْعَامِ الْقَادِمِ؟
I am thinking of studying Music, but I am not sure.	٤٨٦) أُفَكِّرُ فِى دِرَاسَةِ الْمُوسِيقَى وَلَكِنْ غَيْرُ مُتَأَكِّدٍ
Do you like western Music?	٤٨٧) هَلْ تُعْجِبُكَ الْمُوسِيقِيُّ الْغَرْبِيَّةُ؟
No, I prefer classical music	٤٨٨) لاَ ، أُفَضِّلُ الْمُوسِيقِيَّ الْكِلاَسِيكِيَّةَ
Can I speak to Dr. Khalifa?	٤٨٩) هَلْ يُمْكِنُ أَنْ أُكَلِّمَ الدُّكْتُورَ خَلِيفَة؟
Very sorry , It seems I have dialed the wrong number	٤٩٠) أَسِفٌ جِدًّا. يَظْهَرُ اِنِّى اَدَرْتُ قُرْصَ التِّلِفُونِ خَطَأً
The weather is lovely today	٤٩١) اَلْجَوُّ الْيَوْمَ جَمِيلٌ
I want to have my hair cut please	٤٩٢) أُرِيدُ أَنْ أَقُصَّ شَعْرِي مِنْ فَضْلِكَ
I have a surprise for you. A pleasant surprise	٤٩٣) عِنْدِي مُفَاجَأَةٌ لَكَ. مُفَاجَأَةٌ سَارَّةٌ
Are you going to invite me for a dinner with you?	٤٩٤) هَلْ سَتَدْعُونِي إِلَى الْعَشَاءِ مَعَكَ؟

٤٩٥) هَلْ سَتُعْطِينِي هَدِيَّةً؟   Are you going to give me a gift?

٤٩٦) كَانَ الْيَوْم سَعِيدًا فِي حَيَاتِي   Today has been a happy day in my life

٤٩٧) نُرِيدُ شِرَاءَ دِبْلَتَيِنِ لِلْخُطُوبَة   We would like to buy two engagement rings

٤٩٨) تَفَضَّلِي وَ جَرِّبِي هَذِهِ يَا سَيِّدَةُ   Please come and try this , Madam

٤٩٩) أَظُنُّ أَنَّهَا وَاسِعَةٌ قَلِيلاً عَلَى إِصْبَعِي   I think it is a little big for me

٥٠٠) مَا رَأْيُكَ فِى هَذِهِ؟   What do you think of this?

٥٠١) هَذِهِ مُنَاسِبَةٌ تَمَامًا   This suits very well

٥٠٢) نَعَمْ أَرْسَلْتُ لَهُمْ بِطَاقَاتِ تَهْنِئَةٍ   Yes I have sent them greeting cards

٥٠٣) نَسِيتُ أَنْ أُرْسِلَ بِطَاقَاتِ تَهْنِئَةٍ لِصَدِيقِي فِي جُدَّة   I forgot to send a greeting card to my friend in Jeddah

٥٠٤) كَانَتْ زِيَارَتُنَا اِلَى آغْرَا سَعِيدَةً جِدًّا   Our visit to Agra has been very pleasant indeed

٥٠٥) مَتَى يَجِبُ أَنْ نَكُونَ فِى الْمَطَارِ؟   When do we have to be at the airport?

٥٠٦) أُرِيدُ كَشْفَ الْحِسَابِ مِنْ فَضْلِكَ   Could I have the bill, please?

٥٠٧) أَيْنَ أَدْفَعُ الْحِسَابَ؟   Where can I pay the bill?

PART THREE

COMPOSITION

COMPOSITION

(١) مدرستي

هذه مدرستي. مدرستي كبيرة. تقع مدرستي في المدينة الجديدة. اسمها المدرسة الهندية المثالية. هذه مدرسة ثانوية. يدرس فيها حوالي ٤٠٠٠ طالب وطالبة من جنسيات مختلفة.

يتعلم فيهاالطلاب اللغة الانجليزية والعربية فضلا عن اللغة الهندية والاردية. ويتعلمون العلوم والتاريخ والجغرافيا وعلوم الاجتماع والفنون والموسيقى.

تهتم مدرستنا بالتربية الشاملة حيث تمنح الفرص لتوسعة القدرات الذاتية في المجالات المختلفة.

والطلاب يلعبون العابا مختلفة مثل كرة القدم وكرة اليد وكرة السلة وكرة الطائرة وكركت والتنس وغيرها حسب اختيارهم.

فيها مكتبتان كبيرتان. مكتبة للأولاد ومكتبة للبنات. عندنا حصة مكتبية في كل أسبوع ونذهب فيها الى المكتبة لنطالع الكتب ولنقرأ المجلات والجرائد.

وفيها مختبرات حديثة للعلوم ولكمبيوتر للتجارب العلمية والعملية حول القواعد التي ندرسها في الفصول. أحب مدرستي جدا.

(٢) مدرسي

أنا طالب في المدرسة الهندية المثالية. أدرس في الصف العاشر. مدرسي الدكتور عيسى. هو من مصر. هو عالم كبير. وله مؤلفات عديدة في

اللغة العربية والدراسات الاسلامية فضلا عن مقالاته المعاصرة في الجرائد والمجلات المحلية والدولية.

يأتي المدرسة قبل السابعة صباحا ولا يرجع الا في الساعة الثانية بعد الظهر. يعلمنا أمورا دراسية وغير دراسية ويساعدنا على الكتابة والقراءة بارشاداته الرشيدة. أنا أحب مدرسي لأنه رجل صالح ومخلص في أقواله وأفعاله.

مدرسي مولع بالثقافة الاسلامية ويقوم بواجبه في أكمل وجه ممكن. كثيرا ما يشاركنا بفكراته الجذابة وينورنا حل العلم الحديثة حتى نقدر توسيع آفاق تفاهمنا في المواضيع العديدة. مدرسنا مدرس مثالي وأقدم له هذه السطور من الأناشيد العربية :

يا مربي الروح اني	سوف لا انسى الجميلا
أنت حقا أهل كل ال	مكرمات لها دليلا
انت تعلي يوم شأني	أنت تهديني السبيلا
أنت قد فتحت عيني	فاقبل الشكر الجزيلا
عشت للعلياء تبني	عشت استاذي جليلا
صرت ما عاش الكرام	هاديا ظلا ظليلا

(٣) القراءة

الانسان حيوان اجتماعي ويجب عليه أن يقرأ كثيرا ويروي عقله وخياله بالأفكار الطيبة والعلوم النيرة. القراءة عمل نافع نتمتع به ونستفيد منه في حياتنااليومية.

الاسلام دين أشاد بالعلم فاسس بنيانه وأعلى مناره وحسبك ان تكون الآيات الأولى من القرآن الكريم: أقرأ بسم ربك الذي خلق. خلق الانسان من علق. اقرأ وربك الأكرم. الذي علم بالقلم. علم الانسان مالم يعلم.

الانسان الذي يقرأ الكتب المفيدة يجمع من اللؤلؤ من المعرفة والمعلومات والحكمة ويقود المجتمع الى أعلى درجات الثقافة والنهضة الفكرية. وهذا يدل على أهمية القراءة في حياة الانسان ولا بد لنا ان نشجع أولادنا وبناتنا على القراءة المفيدة حتى نقدر ان نبني جيلا حضاريا بفكرات ايجابية.

قراءة الكتب العامة تفيد الطالب معرفته وتوسع مداركه اللغوية كما انها توسع مدارك التفاهم والتعاون بين أعضاء المجتمع.

القرائة هواية جميلة ويجب علينا أن نزرع هذه الهواية في مجتمعنا الحديث.

(٤) المكتبة

المكتبة جزء هام من المجتمع الحضاري الذي يهتم ويفتخر بالثقافة والعلوم. وانه من المزايا المنفردة للانسان.

الانسان من أكرم خلق الله وانعمه الله بقدرات الفهم والتفكر. فلا يشبع الا بالقراءة والكتابة وتبادل الآراء بين أعضاء المجتمع الذي يعيش فيه.

المكتبة مخزن للكتب والجرائد والمجلات. رتبت الكتب والمجلات بطريقة منظمة حسب المواضيع والمؤلفين حتى يسهل الوصول الى العناوين المحتاجة بدون أي مشقة.

توجد المكتبات بالمدارس والكليات والجامعات كما توجد مكتبات عامة في الاماكن المخصصة.

المطالعات والمراجعات المستمرة في المكتبة تجعل الفرد مناسبا لمواجهة تحديات الزمان كما تستعده ان يكون عضوا مثاليا في المجتمع.

علينا ان ننتهز الفرصة للقراءة والتفكر ونستعمل جميع التسهيلات الموجودة لديا لتوسع نطاق تفاهمنا وتعارفنا حتى نقود العالم الى اعلى درجات الثقافة والحضارة.

(٥) رحلة بالطائرة

كنت أتمنى ان اسافر بالطائرة من زمان ولكن لم يتوفر لي فرصة لنيل أملي الا في السنة الماضية حيث أخذني أبي الى الدوحة لزيارة قصيرة خلال أيام عيد الأضحى المبارك.

كانت رحلتي من ممباي الى الدوحة عاصمة دولة قطر مريحة وممتعة. سافرت بطيران الهند وكان رقم الرحلة اي سي ٩٥٧. وكانت هذه الرحلة طويلة حيث استغرقت أكثر من ثلاث ساعات.

كانت الرحلة مدهشة وجميلة. عندما أقلعت الطائرة طلب منا ان نربط حزام الأمان استعدادا للرحلة وخلال دقائق كنا في الجو. قدمت لنا المضيفة الشربات والوجبات الشهية. وكانت الرحلة ممتعة جدا لأسباب عديدة.

هبطت الطائرة في مطارالدوحة الدولي. ونزلنا من الطائرة وسرنا الى مبنى المطارلنخلص الاجراآت اللازمة من قبل الهجرة والجمارك وغيرها.

كان أخي الكبير ينتظرنا في المطار ورحنا معه الى بيته الواقع في المطار القديم. لن انسى هذه الرحلة في حياتي.

(٦) السفر بالقطار

سَافَرتُ في القِطَارِ في الأُسبُوعِ المَاضِي.أَنَا أُسَافِرُ أَوَلَ مَرَّةٍ في القِطَارِ. رَكِبْتُ القِطَارَ الَّذِي يَخْرُجُ مِنْ دَلْهِي وَوَصَلتُ مُمبَاي بَعْدَ سَاعَاتٍ طَوِيلَةٍ.

كَانَ في المَحَطَة صَديقُنَا خَالَدَ هُوَ يَحْجُزُ التَّذْكِرَة لِلرِّحْلَة الَى كَيْرَلا. مَحَطَّةُ القِطار تَعْمَلُ لَيْلَ نَهَار. نَرَى في رَصيف المَحَطَة زَحْمَةً كَثيرَة. بَعْضُ المُسَافِرينَ يَطُوفُونَ أَمَامَ شُبَّاك التَذْكِرَة وَيَسْتَريحُ بَعْضُ المُسَافِرينَ في صَالَة الانتظَار.

القِطَارُ مَرْكَبَةٌ كَبيرَةٌ فيه عَرَبَاتٌ كَثيرَةٌ. بَعْضُ العَرَبَات عَرَبَاتٌ عَامَّةٌ هِيَ لِلرِّحْلَة القَصيرَة وَبَعْضُهَا مَحْجُوزَة وهِيَ لِلرِّحْلَة البَعيدَة.

القِطَارُ أَنواعٌ. قِطَارٌ سَريعٌ وقِطَارٌ مَحَلي وقِطَارُ الأَمتِعَة وغَيرُهَا.

قَابَلتُ صَديقًا لي في السَفَر وفَرِحْتُ بِه كَثيرًا. أَخْبَرَني تَفَاصيلَ عَن أَصدِقَائِنَا الَذينَ دَرَسُوا مَعَنَا في الكُلّية وَتَبَادَلْنَا الهَدَايَا وَالتَهَاني.

وَكَائَتْ هذِه الرِّحْلَةُ مُريحَةٍ وَمُثْمِرَة لأَسْبَاب عَديدَةٍ.

(٧) محطة سكة الحديد

أرأيت محطة سكة الحديد. هي في القرى صغيرة وليس فيها من الأبنية الا محل لناظر المحطة. وهوالرئيس الذي يلاحظ جميع أعمالها. وفيها محل لصرف التذاكر لأن كل مسافر يجب ان تكون في يده تذكرة السفر قبل ان يركب القطار. والتذكرة بطاقة صغيرة من الورق مطبوع عليها اسم المحطة التي يقوم منها المسافر بسفره واسم المحطة التي يريد التوجه اليها ومقدار النول وتاريخ السفر والدرجة التي يركب فيها ورقم القطار وما الى ذلك من البيانات المختلفة.

وفي المدن الكبيرة نرى المحطات واسعة وتستعمل التكنولوجيا الحديثة لاصدار التذاكر وحجزها. محطة القطار تعمل ليل نهار ومزدحمة بالمسافرين والمستودعين والمستقبلين.

PART FOUR

MODEL LETTERS

MODEL LETTERS

(١) طلب الاجازة

سيادة المدرس المكرم

المدرسة الهندية الحديثة، دهلي

تحية طيبة مباركة وبعد،

سيدي المكرم،

أُحيطُكُم علمًا بأني مَريضٌ بالْحُمَّى والزُّكام مُنذُ ثَلاثَة أَيَام وَأَنَا حَالِيًا تَحْتَ مُعَالَجة الطَّبِيب ، انَّهُ نَصَحَني بالاسْتِراحَة لِمُدَة أسْبُوعٍ.

لِذَا أرجُو مِنْ سِيَادَتِكُم الكَرِيمَة التَّفَضُّل بِمَنْحِ الاجَازَة لِتِلْكَ الْمُدَّة، وَشُكْرًا وتَفَضلوا بِقُبُول فَائِق الاحتِرَامِ ،،،

تلميذكم المطيع

التوقيع

الاسم: ....

المكا ن : ....

التاريخ: ....

(٢) طلب اجازة

سيادة المدرس الموقر

المدرسة الهندية المثالية، الدوحة

السلام عليكم ورحمة الله وبركاته وبعد،

اليومَ حَصَلْتُ عَلَى برقية مِنْ صَديقي العَزيز انه يجيئ مِنَ الكُوَيت وَيَصِلُ في السَاعَة التَاسِعَة صَبَاحًا. فَأَرْجُو أَنْ أَذْهَبَ مَعَ عَمِّي الَى المَطَارِ لاسْتِقْبَاله، لِذَا أَطلُبُ مِنْ سِيَادَتِكُم اجَازَةً لهَذا اليَومِ ٢٠٠٥/٤/٢٥

المخلص لكم

التوقيع

الاسم ....

المكان ....

التاريخ ....

(٣) طلب للحصول على قرض من مصرف

التاريخ:

السيد/ المدير العام المحترم

بنك الدوحة المحدود

الدوحة قطر

تحية طيبة وبعد،

يُرجَى التكرم بالعلم بأنَّ شَرِكة أكون للخدمَات شَرِكة ذَاتُ مَسؤُولية مَحْدودة وَتَعمَلُ في الخِدمَات التجَاريَّة المختلفة. حَيثُ انِنَا نُريدُ تَوسِيعَ مَجَال انشِطتَنا أنَّنا في أمَسِّ الحَاجَة الَى تَسهيلات مَصرَفيةٍ اضَافِيةٍ حَتَى نَقْدِر اَن نتم تَوسِيعَ أعمَالنا التجَاريَّة في أقرَبِ وَقْتٍ مُمْكِن.

نَغدُو شَاكِرينَ لَو تَكَرَّمْتُم بِتَزويدِنَا بِمائَة الف دُولاَر اَمريكي قَرْضًا سَنَقُومُ بِتَسديدِه عَلَى دَفْعَات خلاَلَ خَمْسَة أعْوَام مِنْ تَاريخِ مَنْح القرض عِلْمًا بِأنَّا عَلَى استِعْدَاد تَام لِرَهْنِ العَقَارِ الذي تَمْلِكُهُ الشَركَة في شَارِعِ سَلوَى لَدَيكُم ويُقَدَّرُ الثَمَنُ التَقريبي لِهَذَا العَقَار بِحَوَالَي مَليُون دُولار.

وَتَفضلُوا بِقَبُولِ فَائقِ الاحتِرَامِ والتَقْدِير

عن / شركة أكون للخدمات

عبد الشكور أبو بكر

المدير العام

(٤) جواب البنك

التاريخ:

السيد/ عبد الشكور أبوبكر المحترم
مدير عام شركة أكون للخدمات
الدوحة قطر

تحية طيبة وبعد،

نشير الى طلبكم بتاريخ.......... بشأن حصول على قرض اضافي بمبلغ مائة الف دولار ويسرنا ان نحيطكم علما بأننا بعد أن درسنا الأمر بالواضح قررنا منحكم هذا القرض على ان يتم تسديده على دفعات خلال خمسة أعوام.

وبما اننا نعتبر شركتكم من أفضل عملائنا وبالنظر الى العلاقات المتينة الطويلة بيننا قررناعدم مطالبتكم برهن العقارالمشار اليه في طلبكم ويكفينا مانعرفه عنكم من صدق ونزاهة كما و سنكون على استعداد دائم لتقديم أي دعم مالي تحتاجون اليه لتمشية اعمالكم.

متمنيين لشركتكم دوام الازدهار والتوفيق
وتفضلوا بقبول فائق الاحترام

المدير العام
بنك الدوحة المحدودة

(٥) طلب الى المصرف لتحويل مبلغ

التاريخ:

السيد/ مدير بنك قطر الاسلامي   المحترم

الدوحة قطر

تحية طيبة وبعد،

نرجو تحويل خمسة آلاف دولار الى البنك الاسلامي الدولي باسم شركة مطابع أكون رقم الحساب : ٤٩٧٠ ٣٤٥٦٢٣٤ وقيد قيمة التحويل في حسابنا الجاري معكم رقم : ٤٥٧٦٣٤٢

يرجى ارسال الاشعار بالتحويل الى عنواننا المسجل لديكم.

وشكرا

المخلص عبد الشكور أبو بكر

(٦) طلب لتأجيل تسديد قسط التأمين

التاريخ:

السيد/ مدير شركة التأمين الاسلامية المحترم
الدوحة قطر

بعد التحية،

استلمت رسالتكم في تاريخ ٢٠٠٥/٥/٢٤ ونود أن نعلمكم انه بسبب الظروف المالية التي لم أتوقع حصولها لن أتمكن من تسديد القسط الذي يستحق قبل نهاية هذا الشهر. آمل بأن أقوم بالتسديد في نهاية شهر يولو القادم.

هل يمكنكم ان تمنحوني فرصة السماح هذه علما بأني على اتم الاستعداد لدفع الفائدة التي تستحق على هذا التأخير في التسديد.
وتفضلوا بقبول فائق الاحترام،،

أمان الله محمد العالمي

(٧) طلب لارسال المسؤول لتقييم خسارة الحريق

التاريخ:

السيد/ مدير شركة قطر

للتأمين واعادة التأمين المحترم

الدوحة قطر

تحية طيبة وبعد،

نأسف لاعلامكم بأن حريقا شد في مستودعاتنا الواقعة في طريق سلوى في الساعة الثانية من صباح هذا اليوم وقد لاحظ الحارس الليلي لمستودعاتنا حدوث الحريق فاتصل فورا بفرقة الاطفاء التي جاء أفرادها الى مكان الحريق بنصف ساعة ولم تتمكن فرقة الاطفاء من اخماد الحريق تماما الا عند الساعة الرابعة بعد ان اتى الحريق على كامل محتويات المستودعات.

ان تقديرنا الأولى للخسائر هو بحوالي مليون دولار ونطلب منكم ان ترسلوا المسؤول عن تقدير الخسار من اجل اجراء التقييم النهائي للأضرار الحاصلة. وتفضلوا بقبول فائق الاحترام ،،،

عن/ شركة قطر الوطنية

المدير

(٨) رسالة صديق الى صديقه بمناسبة الزواج

عزيزي أحمد،

السلام عليكم ورحمة الله وبركاته وبعد،

سررت جدا عندما علمت بأنك تنوي الزواج قريبا من فتاة أحلامك. وقد وصلتني بالفعل دعوتك لحضور حفل الزواج الذي سأحضره بالطبع رغم بعد المساحة التي تفصل بيننا.

وانتهز هذه الفرصة لأدعو الله عز وجل ان يوفق على هذا واتمنى لك كل الحظ والامتنان في حياتك الزوجية.

صديقك المخلص

أمان الله

(٩) رسالة شكر على معونة مالية

عزيزي خالد،

السلام عليكم ورحمة الله وبركاته وبعد،

استلمت مع الشكر الجزيل حوالتك البريدية بمبلغ الف دولار وجاءت هذه المساعدة في وقتها تماما لأنه كان علي كما أخبرتك في رسالتي السابقة تسديد الأقساط المدرسية كما يجب علي تسديد قرض البنك.

تأكد يا خالد بأني سأسدد لك هذا المبلغ في أقرب فرصة ممكنة ولن تتجاوز فترة التسديد ستة أشهر بمشيئة الله وتوفيقه. لقد أثبت انك الصديق الوفي المخلص فالصديق يكون في وقت الضيق كما يقول المثل.

أشكرك مرة أخرى وآمل أن تمنح لي فرصة في المستقبل لرد صنيعك بأجمل منه.

صديقك المخلص

عبد الله

(١٠) رسالة شكر على الضيافة

عزيزي فضل الرحمن،
السلام عليكم ورحمة الله وبركاته وبعد،

أغتنم فرصة العودة الى الوطن لأقدم لك ولزوجتك الأخت صفية باسمي
واسم زوجتي خالص شكرنا وتقديرنا للضيافة الكريمة التي قمتما بها تجاهنا في
زيارتنا لمدينتكم وللأيام الممتعة التي قضيناها سوية.

كانت فرصة اللقاء عزيزة علينا وتمتعنا بصحبتكما بأيام جميلة لن ننساها
ولكن عليكما ان لا تنسيا وعدكما لنا بزيارتنا في الصيف المقبل لكي نجدد
متعة اللقاء والمحبة

ودمت لصديقك

أمان الله

PART FIVE

POEMS PRESCRIBED
FOR STD 9 AND 10

POEMS PRESCRIBED FOR STD 9

(١) المذياع

هـــو في الحيـــاة مرفـــه ومنعم   ومعلم ينبيــك مـــا لا تعلـــم

يطوي بك الدنيا وانك هاهــنا   لم تنتقـــل فكأن راسك يحلـــم

من كل ارجاء البـــلاد حـــديثه   وبكل السنة الـــورى يتـكلم

وكم سمعنا في المساء وفي الضحى   شخصا عـــلى بعد النوى يترنم

عجبا لمعجزة العـــلوم وفضـــلها   كـــم للعلـــوم على البـــرية أنعـــم

Word meanings:

enjoying	منعم	entertainer	مرفه	life	حياة
you know	تعلم	inform	ينبأ	teacher	معلم
dreams	يحلم	move	تنتقل	cover	يطوي
creature	ورى	tongues	السنة	parts	ارجاء
forenoon	ضحى	evening	مساء	speak	يتكلم
wonder	عجب	singing	يترنم	far away	بعد
		greatness	فضل	sciences	علوم

(٢) الطائر

وليــس فيــه طـربــي	الحـبـس ليـس مــذهبي
وان يــكن مــن ذهــب	فلست ارضــى قـفصا
والعيش فيهـا مطلبـي	غابـات ربـي غـايتي
وراق فيهـا مــشربي	قـد طـاب فيها مطعمي
مــن ماء نـبع أعــذب	أذهـب فيـها أستـقـي
فالـحبس ليـس مذهـي	أصـدح فيها مـطلـقا

Word meanings

happiness	طرب	way	مذهب	imprisonment	حبس
gold	ذهب	cage	قفص	satisfied	ارضى
live	عيش	aim	غاية	forests	غابات
eating place	مطعم	to be good	طاب	requirement	مطلب
I go	اذهب	drinking place	مشرب	to be good	راق
spring	نبع	water	ماء	I drink	استقي
without any control	مطلق	I shout	اصدح	pure	اعذب

(٣) ترنيمة الولد في الصباح

ولــى الظــلام هــاربا	أشرقـت الشمـس وقـد
شـكرا عظـيما واجـبا	فالشـكر لله ٱلأحــد
الأمور باسمه	مـا أحـسن النـور أرى فيه

147

والطيــر تشــدو سحـرا   على   الغصون   قائمه

مــا أحـسـن النــور البهي   فيه   اجد   عاملا

انـــي اود دائمـــا   الا   أكون   خاملا

الله قــد أجـارنـي   من كل شر في الظلام

شــكـرا لـه قــد صـانـي   شكــرا لــه على الـدوام

Word meanings

go back	ولى	sun	شمس	sunrise	أشرق
thanks	شكر	run away	هارب	darkness	ظلام
light	نور	compulsory	واجب	great	عظيم
bird	طير	smiling	باسمه	things	امور
branches	غصون	with out sleeping	سحرا	sings	تشدو
I work hard	اجد	beautiful	بهي	standing	قائمه
always	دائم	I like	اود	work	عامل
evil	شر	saved	اجار	lazy	خامل
		always	دوام	protected	صان

(٤) ترنيمة الأم للصبي في المساء

ان الفراش الناعما   فيه   تنام   دائما

نم يا حبيب سالما   نم   آمنا نم   آمنا

راح النهار واحتجب   معه   العناء   والتعب

148

نم آمنا نم آمنا نم بالأمن اقترب والليل

في حفظ مولانا الصمد عصافير الغرد باتت

نم في حماه آمنا من ليس يغفل عن أحد

من كل ضيم أو كدر نم آمنا حتى السحر

نم في حماه آمنا نم في حمى بارئ البشر

Word meanings

you sleep	تنام	soft	ناعم	bed	فراش
peacefully	آمنا	safely	سالما	darling	حبيب
got covered	احتجب	day	نهار	went	راح
night	ليل	tiredness	تعب	problems	عناء
spend the night	بات	come close	اقترب	security	أمن
protection	حفظ	singing	غرد	sparrows	عصافير
protection	حمى	unaware	يغفل	omnipotent	الصمد
problem	كدر	difficulty	ضيم	dawn	سحر
				Creator of mankind	بارئ البشر

(٥) الفأر

بل يختبئ في داخل الأجحار الفأر لا يخرج في النهار

وكان أهل البيت فيه ناموا لكنه اذا أتى الظلام

يأكل ما شاء من الطعام يسرح في البيت بلا احتشام

النفائسا يحرمنا وتارة فتارة يأكل خبزا يابسا

أم من حليب طيب أو سمن من عجوة او زبدة أو جبن

غادر طيب العيش في الدار وفر ثم اذا أحس باهر ظهر

من دون أن تأخذه ندامة يلتمس النجاة والسلامة

Word meanings

hides	يختبئ	come out	يخرج	rat	فأر
roam around	يسرح	holes	اجحار	inside	داخل
bread	خبز	sometimes	تارة	modesty	احتشام
precious things	نفائس	spoils	يحرم	dry	يابس
ghee	جبن	butter	زبدة	cheese	عجوة
felt	أحس	ghee	سمن	milk	حليب
leave	غادر	appeared	ظهر	cat	هر
safety	نجاة	search	يلتمس	run	فر
		sorrow	ندامة	safety	سلامة

(٦) الطائر والبنات

بمــحيـاك وسهــلا البنات : أيها الطائر أهلا

الهديل ذاك زانه فقت كل الطير شكلا

والدينا من خبرا غننا وأقرأ علينا

الجميلا نرعى اننا تسد معروفا الينا

الطائر: أمكن استودعتني شوقها اذ ودعتني

وكـتابـا حـملتـني لفظه يشفي العليل

انني عنكن ذاهب والى الأوطان آئب

راجيا حسن العواقب من لدن رب جليل

البنات: أيها الراحل عنا لك خير الشكر منا

سر الى الأوطان انا قد أذنا بالرحيل

اقرأ يا خير الحمام امنـا منـا السـلام

ذاك أقصى ما يرام وبـه تـم الـجـميـل

POEMS PRESCRIBED FOR STD 10

(٧) النحلة والزنبار

الألفاظ الصعبة:

الزنبار رضاب شهد العليل العويل

اعتداء الشقاء خدعة طرا

الزنبار : أنت يا نحلة ماذا يشغل الناس بحبك

انني في حسن شكلي لست محبوبا كحبك

انظري مني جمالا زانه لون عجيب

كيف لا يعشق مثلي؟ ان هذا لغريب!

النحلة: في رضابي حلو شهد يشتفي منه العليل

ليس للزنبار نفع فعلام ذا العويل

151

شرا   تستر   خدعة   ان حسن الشكل هذا

طرا   عند أهل الأرض   ذميم   كل   خداع

واعتداء   شرور   او   حسن شكل فيه ضر

الشقاء   ياتي   به   بل   ليس يرجى منه حب

Word meanings:

engage	يشغل	honey bee	نحلة	wasp	زنبار
loved	محبوب	حسن شكل good appearance		love	حب
decorated	زان	beauty	جمال	look	انظر
loved	يعشق	wonderful	عجيب	colour	لون
saliva	رضاب	strange	غريب	like	مثل
cures	يشتفي	honey	شهد	sweetness	حلو
howling	عويل	benefit	نفع	sick	عليل
evil	شر	hides	تستر	cheating	خدعة
all	طرا	condemned	ذميم	cheater	خداع
enmity	اعتداء	evils	شرور	evil	ضر
		misfortune	شقاء	expect	يرجى

(٢) ولا تصنع المعروف في غير أهله

لئيم   احذر   قط   يبقى   رمد   طائش

لقد رمد الثعبان يوما من الشتى   فمر   غلام   واستعد   لنقله

وجاء بع يسعى الى الدار طائشا   وأدفأه   فانظر   لقلة   عقله

فلما أحس الوحش بالدفئ حوله   وساحت سموم الموت في الجسم كله

وفتح   عينيه   وحرك   رأسه   على الولد المسكين يبغي لقتله

أتاه أبوه عاجلا قط رأسه   وداس عليه غاضبا بنعاله

وقال بني احذر لئيما لقيته   ولا تصنع المعروف في غير اهله

Word meanings:

unable to see	رمد	good	معروف	do	تصنع
walked	مر	winter	شتاء	snake	ثعبان
move	نقل	got ready	استعد	boy	غلام
house	دار	running	يسعى	came	جاء
lack of	قلة	heated	ادفأ	exhausted	طائش
beast	وحش	felt	احس	intelligence	عقل
spread	ساح	around	حول	warmth	دفئ
body	جسم	death	موت	poison	سموم
killed	قتل	want	يبغي	all	كل
cut	قط	hurriedly	عاجل	came	اتى
angrily	غاضباً	stamped	داس	head	راس
condemned	لئيم	beware of	احذر	slipper	نعال
				meet	لقي

(٣) جزاء الوالدين

لشم	حنين	شاحب	أواه	مهد
نبض	البرء	وقع	ضجة	هتف
	حنان	الغمم		السقم

ورقدت في مهدي وكم أشكو وكم	مالي مرضت وكم أقاسي من الم
هتفت يا أماه قالت لي نعم	اواه من وجع أراه أصابني
وحنين صوت هاج من قلب لفم	جائت على عجل بلون شاحب
وجاءت تجيئ بما يخفف لي الألم	لثمت خدودي رحمة ومحبة
وتقص من خبر البلاد مع الأمم	عادت تسليني بعذب حديثها
وكلام أشخاص فوقعا بالقدم	حتى سمعت على السلام ضجة
هو ذا الطبيب لكي يعالجني قدم	هذا ابي وبجنبه رجل أتى
ورجا لى البرء السريع من السقم	قاس الحرارة جس نبضي بعدها
مرا ولكن فيه كشف للغمم	حضر الدواء فشربته فوجدته
فنشطت حتى من سروري لم انم	فرحت لذا أمي وداعبني أبي
وكذاك حب أبي فما هذي النعم	هذا حنان الأم من أجل ابنها
ومحبة ما شاء ربي ذو الكرم	لجزاء هذا الحب مني طاعة

Word meanings

pain	الم	I suffer	اقاسي	be sick	مرض
I complain	اشكو	cradle	مهد	slept	رقد
shouted	هتف	affected	اصاب	pain	وجع
fade	شاحب	hurriedly	عجل	said	قال

raise	هاج	sound	صوت	affection	حنين
touch	لثم	mouth	فم	heart	قلب
love	محبة	mercy	رحمة	cheek	خدود
console	تسلي	reduce	يخفف	run	جرى
tell	تقص	talk	حديث	sweat	عذب
societies	امم	countries	بلاد	news	خبر
sound	ضجة	staircase	سلالم	heard	سمع
foot	قدم	persons	اشخاص	talk	كلام
treat	يعالج	man	رجل	side	جنب
temperature	حرارة	measured	قاس	came	قدم
wished, hoped	رجا	pulse	نبض	check	جس
disease	سقم	fast	سريع	recovery	برء
drank	شرب	medicine	دواء	brought	حضر
relief	كشف	bitter	مرا	found	وجد
play	داعب	became happy	فرح	difficulty	غمم
affection	حنان	happiness	سرور	became active	نشط
				obedience	طاعة

(٤) رجال المطافي

ابطال	اللظى	عدة	الفضاء
	الودود	كهل	العطب

قد كنت في احدى الليالي ماشيا   والبدر في أعلى الفضاء زاهيا

كان يشكو لي رفيقي حاله   حتى بلغنا شارع الفجالة

ولم يكد يأتي صديقي مثله   حتى سمعنا ضجة وزلزلة

فقلت ما ذلك يا رفيقي   فقال تلك عدة الحريق

ولم نكد نتم بعد قولنا   حتى رأينا الكل صار حولنا

أبصرت فيما بينهم رجالا   رجال بأس في اللظى أبطالا

يخاطرون بالنفوس في اللهب   لينقذوا غيرهم من العطب

كم أنقذوا من عاجز وطفل   وامرأة مسنة وكهل

وكم حموا من أنفس المتاع   ما صار لولاهم الى الضياع

فهم وان كانو من الانسان   عزمهم أمضى من النيران

لهم حنان المشفق الودود   كما لهم جزاءه الاسود

Word meanings

high	اعلى	moon	بدر	walking	ماشي
reached	بلغ	shining	زاهي	space	فضاء
shaking	زلزلة	house	منزل	street, road	شارع
fire	حريق	equipment	عدة	friend	رفيق
saw	ابصر	became	صار	we complete	نتم
heroes	ابطال	fire	لظى	strength	باس
save	ينقذ	flame	لهب	endanger	يخاطر
lady	امرأة	old	عاجز	decay	عطب
protected	حمى	middle aged	كهل	aged	مسنة
determination	عزم	waste	ضياع	goods	متاع
affectionate	المشفق	fire	نيران	sharper	أمضى
big	الاسود	reward	جزاء	loving	ودود

PART SIX

MODEL QUESTION PAPERS

MODEL QUESTION PAPER
C.B.S.E March 2001 Examination

1. Define and illustrate any two of the following terms with examples. (10 marks)

مفعول به، اسم ان وأخواقا، ضمير مرفوع منفصل، تثنية، حروف عطف، جملة فعلية، جمع سالم

2. Translate any five of the following sentences into English or Urdu or Hindi (10 marks)

١) ساعتكم رخيصة جدا

٢) أنتم تذهبون الى المدرسة

٣) لم يفتح أخي بابا

٤) كم ساعة يقرأ أخوك في البيت ؟

٥) سوهن وموهن طالبان ذكيان

٦) دخل أبوكما ثم أمكما الغرفة

٧) هذان القميصان جديدان

٨) ذلك الولد نجح في الامتحان

3. Translate any five of the following sentences into Arabic (10 marks)

   1. How do you write this name?

   2. Where is your house?

   3. They (women) want two books.

4. You have three vehicles

5. After prayer we will go to the market

6. Do not play in this ground

7. My school is in the old city

8. The two papers are on the table

4. Use any five of the following words in simple sentences (10 marks)

لست، رجعتم، قديمان، طالبتان، الأجوبة، المدرسون، لن، لم،
أمسى، ليت

5. Write a short paragraph in Arabic on any one of the following topics. (10)

حديقتي، تاج محل، السفر بالقطار، صديقي

6. Translate any two of the following passages into English, or Urdu or Hindi (35 marks)

(١)

مريم: السلام عليكم كيف حالك يا أمي ، وكيف حالك يا أخي

الأم : وعليكم السلام ، أهلا يا بنتي. متى خرجت من المدرسة؟.

مريم: خرجت بعد صلاة الظهر

الأم : أين زميلاتك آمنة وفاطمة وسعاد ؟

مريم: أنا ما رأيتهن بعد الصلاة.

الام: يا بنتي أخوك حفظ صورة الرحمن. أي سورة حفظت انت؟

مريم : أنا حفظت سورة الحديد. وهي أطول من سورة الرحمن. وكذلك
حفظت ست عشرة آية من سورة النساء

(٢)

الأب : ماذا تريدين انت يا حفصة؟

حفصة: أريد حقيبة

الأب : أما عندك حقيبة ؟

حفصة: بلى ، عندي حقيبة حمراء وأريد حقيبة أخرى سوداء

الأب : ماذا تريدين يا سعاد ؟

سعاد: عندي مسطرة صغيرة ، أريد أخرى كبيرة

الاب: وماذا تريدين انت يا ليلى ؟

ليلى : أريد مصحفا ذا حرف كبير

الأب : أما تريدين شيئا يا سلمى ؟

سلمى: بلى ، أريد معجما انجليزيا وأخرى فرنسيا.

(٣)

المدرس : أشكركم يا إخوان.... كم طالبا في فصلكم هذا؟

عمر : فيه أربعون طالبا

المدرس : ولكني أرى خمسة وثلاثين طالبا فقط. فأين الآخرون؟

عمر : هم غائبون اليوم

المدرس : أي كتاب تقرأون ؟

عدنان : نقرأ هذا الكتاب. اسمه قصص النبيين

المدرس : لمن هو ؟

عدنان : هو لفضيلة الشيخ أبي الحسن الندوي

المدرس : كم صفحة قرأتم فيه ؟

جعفر : قرأنا ثلاثا وخمسين صفحة.

عدنان : الكتاب فيه تسعون صفحة. قرأنا منها ثلاثا وخمسين صفحة فبقي سبع وثلاثون صفحة.

7. Explain any one of the following verses in English or Urdu or Hindi (15 marks)

(الف)

فعلام ذا العويل	النحلة: ليس للزنبار نفع
هذا خدعة تستر شرا	ان حسن الشكل
عند أهل الأرض طرا	كل خداع ذمم
أو شرور واعتداء	حسن شكل فيه ضر
بل به يأتي الشقاء	ليس يرجى منه حب

(ب)

ورجا لي البرء السريع من السقم	قاس الحرارة جس نبضي بعدها
مرا ، ولكن فيه كشف للغمم	حضر الدواء فشربته فوجدته
فنشطت حتى من سروري لم أنم	فرحت لذا أمي وداعبني أبي
كذاك حب أبي فماهذي النعم	هذا حنان الأم منأجلابنها
ومحبة ما شاء ربي ذو الكرم	لجزاء هذا الحب مني طاعة

161

C.B.S.E MARCH 2002 Examination

1. Define and illustrate any two of the following terms with examples. (10 marks)

ماضي معروف، اسم كان وأخواتها، مفعول له، ضمير مرفوع متصل، جزم الفعل المضارع ، جمع مؤنث، السالم ، مفعول معه

2. Translate any five of the following sentences into English or Urdu or Hindi (10 marks)

١ . أذهب الى المدرسة اليوم

٢ . تقرئين القرآن ثم تصلين

٣ . البنات فتحن كتبهن

٤ . اشترينا الساعات الجديدة أمس

٥ . كان الحر شديدا في بلدي

٦ . ان الله غفور رحيم

٧ . ليس الباب مغلقا

٨ . لن تنام على هذين السريرين

3. Translate any five of the following sentences into Arabic (10 marks)

1. Will you (two men) read this book?

2. Are you (fem. pl.) students of that college?

3. He became teacher in the old school.

4. They (mas. pl.) will never succeed in the examination.

5. They never attend the class.

6. When will the new shop open?

7. They (fem. pl.) read Quran every day

8. How many rupees do you want?

4. Use any five of the following words in simple sentences (10 marks)

المستشفى، حصة، الصحف، مكتب، من، أكبر، صار، المكتبتان،
اللغة العربية، نصف ساعة

5. Write a short paragraph in Arabic on any one of the following topics. (10 marks)

السفر بالباص، حديقة الحيوانات، مدرستي، المسجد الجامع بدلهي

6. Translate any two of the following passages into English, or Urdu or Hindi (35 marks)

(١)

أحمد: كم طالبا في فصلكم يا علي ؟

علي: في فصلنا أربعة عشر طالبا.

أحمد: الطلاب في فصلنا أكثر. فيه تسعة عشر طالبا. يا علي ما اسم
الطالب الجديد الذي جاء أمس ؟

علي: اسمه أسامة.

أحمد: هو طويل جدا. أليس كذلك ؟

علي: بلى هو طويل جدا ولكن حامدا أطول منه. انه أطول طالب في فصلنا ومن هو أطول طالب في فصلكم ؟

أحمد: أطول طالب في فصلنا ابراهيم.

علي: أدفترك هذا يا أحمد ؟ ان خطك جميل جدا ما شاء الله.

أحمد: شكرا يا علي. خطي جميل وخطك أجمل.

(٢)

يعقوب: يا استاذ عندي سؤال ليست له علاقة بالدرس.

المدرس: ما هو؟

يعقوب: قرأت في كتاب ان النجوم أبعد من الشمس. أصحيح هذا؟

المدرس: نعم ، هذا صحيح...

المدرس: مم خلق الله الانسان يا عثمان؟

عثمان : خلق الله الانسان من طين.

المدرس: أحسنت يا عثمان.

المدرس: ومم خلق الله الجان يا ابا بكر؟

أبو بكر: خلق الله الجان من نار.

المدرس: كيف عرفت ذلك يا أبا بكر؟

ابو بكر: عرفت ذلك من القرآن الكريم. فجاء في سورة الأعراف أن ابليس قال لله : أنا خير منه خلقتني من نار وخلقته من طين "

(٣)

المدرس: الا تريد ان تذهب الى بلدك ؟

يوسف: نعم لا أريد ان اذهب الى بلدي هذه السنة. اريد أن أذهب الى لندن لأدرس اللغة الانجليزية هناك.

المدرس : ألا يمكنك أن تدرس اللغة الانجليزية في بلدك؟

يوسف: نعم لا يمكنني ذلك لأن أهل بلدي يدرسون اللغة الفرنسية ولا يدرسون اللغة الانجليزية.

المدرس: في أي كلية تريد أن تدرس في العام المقبل يا مروان ؟

مروان: أريد أن أدرس في كلية الشريعة.

7. Explain any one of the following verses in English or Urdu or Hindi (15 marks)

(الف)

فمر غلام واستعد لنقله	لقد رمد الثعبان يوما من الشتا
وأدفأه فانظر لقلة عقله	وجاء به يسعى الى الدار طائشا
وساحت سموم الموت في الجسم كله	فلما أحس الوحش بالدفء حوله
على الولد المسكين يبغي لقتله	وفتح عينيه وحرك رأسه
وداس عليه غاضبا بنعاله	أتاه أبوه عاجلا قط رأسه

(ب)

يمشي على رجليه باعتدال	كان الغراب في الزمان الخالي
وقد دهى عقل الغراب العجب	فأبصر العصفور يوما يلعب
وقفزه حين مشى وفاته	فلم يزل يستحسن التفاته
وطيره ووثبه وخفته	وفكر الغراب في تلفته
وحاول الخروج من حدوده	وأكد العزم على تقليده

165

C.B.S.E MARCH 2003 Examination

1. Define and illustrate any two of the following terms with
    examples. (10 marks)

ماضي معروف، اسم كان وأخواتها، مفعول له، ضمير مرفوع متصل،
جزم الفعل المضارع، جمع مؤنث السالم، مفعول معه

2. Translate any five of the following sentences into English
    or Urdu or Hindi (10 marks)

١. هذان أخوان.

٢. دكانكم قريب جدا.

٣. رأيت محطة سكة الحديد في دلهي القديمة.

٤. هل رأيتم الطائرة؟

٥. نعم رأيتها في مدراس.

٦. كم غرفة في بيتكن؟

٧. متى يذهب أخوك الى ممباي؟

٨. أبونا معلم في هذه المدرسة.

3. Translate any five of the following sentences into Arabic
    (10 marks)

    1. How do you write this name?

    2. Where is his school in the city?

    3. They (women) want two books.

    4. Arabic language is the language of the Quran.

    5. You have three houses.

    6. Do your teachers know Arabic?

166

7. Do not enter these rooms.

8. Do not play in this ground(to a girl)

4. Use any five of the following words in simple sentences (10 marks)

تنامون، الكتب الجديدة، المجلات، الشاي، رئيس الهند، السبوة، تردن، مفتوحة، ذلك الكتاب، الحمد

5. Write a short paragraph in Arabic on any one of the following topics. (10 marks)

القلعة الحمراء ، مدرسي ، المكتبة ، عيد الفطر

6. Translate any two of the following passages into English, or Urdu or Hindi (35 marks)

(١)

هشام : أنا مدرس جديد بالجامعة. اسمي هشام. انا من الولايات المتحدة.

بلال : أهلا وسهلا ومرحبا بك يا أخي. أنا مسرور بلقائك. أنا زميلك. اسمي بلال بن حامد. أمن واشنطن أنت يا هشام.

هشام : لا ، أنا لست من واشنطن. اني من نيويورك.

بلال : أمسلم أبوك يا هشام؟

هشام : لا ، هو ليس بمسلم.

بلال : وأمك أ مسلمة هي ؟

بلال: لا هي ليست بمسلمة.

(٢)

دخل المدرس الفصل ووجد فيه خمسة عشر طالبا فقط. فقال لهم: أين الطلاب الجدد الخمسة الذين جاءوا أمس ؟

عبد الله : حضروا اليوم. وخرجو قبل قليل. أظن أنهم ذهبوا الى المدير.

رجع الطلاب الخمسة قبل قليل، فقال لهم المدرس: أالى المدير ذهبتم يا أبنائي؟

قالو : نعم ذهبنا اليه لأنا ماوجدنا أسمائنا في القائمة.

جلس المدرس وقال : اقرأتم درس الأمس يا أبنائي ؟

قال الطلاب : نعم قرأنا و كتبنا وحفظنا

(٣)

المدرس: ألا يمكنك أن تدرس اللغة الانجليزية في بلدك؟

يوسف: نعم لا يمكنني ذلك لأن أهل بلدي يدرسون اللغة الفرنسية ولا يدرسون اللغة الانجليزية.

المدرس: في أي كلية تريد أن تدرس في العام المقبل يا مروان ؟

مروان: أريد أن أدرس في كلية الشريعة.

المدرس: في أي كلية تريد ان تدرس أنت يا موسى.

7. Explain any one of the following verses in English or Urdu or Hindi (15 marks)

(الف)

قاس الحرارة جس نبضي بعدها   ورجا لي البرء السريع من السقم

حضر الدواء فشربته فوجدته   مرا، ولكن فيه كشف للغمم

168

فرحت لذا أمي وداعبني أبي   فنشطت حتى من سروري لم أنم

هذا حنان الأم من أجل ابنها   كذاك حب أبي فماهذي النعم

لجزاء هذا الحب مني طاعة   محبة ما شاء ربي ذو الكرم

(ب)

النحلة : ليس للزنبار نفع   فعلام ذا العويل

ان حسن الشكل   هذا خدعة تستر شرا

كل خداع ذميم   عند أهل الأرض طرا

حسن شكل فيه ضر   أو شرور واعتداء

ليس يرجى منه حب   بل به يأتي الشقاء

CBSE MARCH 2004 Examination

1. Define and illustrate any two of the following terms with examples. (10 marks)

مفعول به، اسم كان صار، مفعول فيه، حروف عطف، ضمير منصوب متصل، جمع مذكر السالم

2. Translate any five of the following sentences into English or Urdu or Hindi (10 marks)

١ . متى يعود أبوك من ايران ؟

٢ . هما طالبان ذكيان

٣ . موهن أطول طالب في الفصل

٤ . هناك ألف روبية في كيسي

٥ . فيصل ماكتب الأجوبة لأن قلمه مكسور

٦ . مُدرِّسي رجل طيب جدا

٧ . مرحبا بكم أيهاالمدرسون

٨ . الشمس تطلع من المشرق

3. Translate any five of the following sentences into Arabic (10 marks)

   1. Is this pen from India?

   2. You are an intelligent and hard working student.

   3. How many brothers do you have?

   4. Quran is the book of Allah.

5. The principal is in his room.

6. I have one thousand rupees.

7. In this school, one hundred students are from Afghanistan.

8. They (two men) are new teachers in the college.

4. Use any five of the following words in simple sentences (10 marks)

ذهبن، لم، اليوم، لن، كان، المكتبة، ان، فتحتم، المدارس، كتابان

5. Write a short paragraph in Arabic on any one of the following topics. (10 marks)

مدرسي، سوق القرية، القلعة الحمراء، حديقة الحيوانات

6. Translate any two of the following passages into English, or Urdu or Hindi (35 marks)

(الف)

المدرس: يا أختر، سمعت أن أخاك طبيب شهير، ويأتيه المرضى من جميع أنحاء باكستان. أصحيح هذا؟

أختر   : هذا صحيح يا فضيلة الشيخ.

المدرس : ياعثمان، اذهب الى المكتبة وهات الجزأ الثالث من (لسان العرب)

هاشم : يا فضيلة الشيخ، أظن أن لسان العرب معجم.

المدرس : نعم هو معجم كبير في ٢٠ جزء

هاشم : لمن هو يا فضيلة الشيخ؟

المدرس : هو لابن منظور

171

(ب)

يوسف : نعم لا أريد أن أذهب الى بلدي هذه السنة اريد ن أذهب الى لندن لأدرس اللغة الانكليزية هناك

المدرس : ألا يمكنك أن تدرس اللغة الانكليزية في بلدك؟

يوسف : نعم لا يمكنني ذلك لأن أهل بلدي يدرسون اللغة الفرنسية ولا يدرسون اللغة الانجليزية.

المدرس : في أي كلية تريد أن تدرس في العام المقبل يا مروان ؟

مروان : أريد أن أدرس في كلية الشريعة.

(ج)

دخل المدرس الفصل ووجد فيه خمسة عشر طالبا فقط. فقال لهم: أين الطلاب الجدد الخمسة الذين جاءوا أمس؟

عبد الله : حضروا اليوم. وخرجو قبل قليل. أظن أنهم ذهبواالى المدير.

رجع الطلاب الخمسة قبل قليل، فقال لهم المدرس: أالى المديرذهبتم يا أبنائي؟

قالو : نعم ذهبنا اليه لأنا ماوجدنا أسمائنا في القائمة.

جلس المدرس وقال : اقرأتم درس الأمس يا أبنائي ؟

قال الطلاب : نعم قرأنا و كتبنا وحفظنا

7. Explain any one of the following verses in English or Urdu or Hindi (15 marks)

(الف)

الزنبار:

بحبك	الناس	يشغل	ماذا	نحلة	يا	أنت
بحبك	محبوبا	لست	شكلي	حسن	في	اني

172

انظري مني جمالا زانه لون عجيب

كيف لا يعشق مثلي ان هذا لغريب

النحلة:

في رضابي حلو شهد يشتفي منه العليل

(ب)

مالي مرضت وكم أقاسي من ألم ورقدت في مهدي وكم أشكو وكم

أواه من وجع أراه أصابني فهتفت يا أماه قالت لي نعم

جاءت على عجل بلون شاحب وحنين صوت هاج من قلب لفم

لثمت خدودي رحمة ومحبة وجرت تجيء بما يخفف لي الألم

عادت تسليني بعذب حديثها وتقص بخبر البلاد مع الأمم

173

C.B.S.E MARCH 2005 Examination

1. Define and illustrate any two of the following terms with examples. (10 marks)

اسم كان وأخواتها، ضمير مرفوع متصل، المضارع المنصوب، النون الثقيلة في المضارع، الفاعل، حروف جوازم المضارع.

2. Translate any five of the following sentences into English or Urdu or Hindi (10 marks)

١. أنتما مدرسان في المدرسة

٢. هما يسكنان في دهلي القديمة

٣. أخي يعمل في المصنع

٤. من سافر الى آغراه ؟

٥. اللغة العربية جميلة جدا

٦. بكم اشترين هذا القلم ؟

٧. ثمنه خمس روبيات

٨. لن نذهب الى تلك الحديقة

3. Translate any five of the following sentences into Arabic (10 marks)

1. Did you read this book?

2. It is a book on Indian history.

3. It is prescribed in our course.

4. The railway station is near our college.

5. Did you travel by train?

6. When our friend came we received him.

7. They play football every day.

8. Our college is the best.

4. Use any five of the following words in simple sentences (10 marks)

جميلة ، تابوا ، اشتريت ، الى ، هن ، لن ، الهند ، السوق ، من ، عامل

5. Write a short paragraph in Arabic on any one of the following topics. (10 mrks)

مدرسي ، ملعب الكلية ، منارة قطب ، محطة سكة الحديد

6. Translate any two of the following passages into English, or Urdu or Hindi (35 marks)

(١)

هشام : أنا مدرس جديد بالجامعة. اسمي هشام. انا من الولايات المتحدة.

بلال : أهلا وسهلا ومرحبا بك يا أخي. أنا مسرور بلقائك. أنا زميلك.
اسمي بلال بن حامد. أمن واشنطن أنت يا هشام.

هشام : لا ، أنا لست من واشنطن. اني من نيويورك.

بلال : أمسلم أبوك يا هشام؟

هشام : لا ، هو ليس بمسلم.

بلال : وأمك أمسلمة هي ؟

هشام : لا هي ليست بمسلمة.

(٢

دخل المدرس الفصل ووجد فيه خمسة عشر طالبا فقط. فقال لهم: أين الطلاب الجدد الخمسة الذين جاءوا أمس ؟

عبدالله : حضروا اليوم. وخرجو قبل قليل. أظن أنهم ذهبوا الى المدير.

رجع الطلاب الخمسة قبل قليل، فقال لهم المدرس: أالى المدير ذهبتم يا أبنائي؟

قالوا : نعم ذهبنا اليه لأنا ما وجدنا أسماءنا في القائمة.

جلس المدرس وقال : اقرأتم درس الأمس يا أبنائي ؟

الطلاب : نعم قرأنا و كتبنا وحفظنا

(٣

المدرس: ألا يمكنك أن تدرس اللغة الانجليزية في بلدك؟

يوسف : نعم لا يمكنني ذلك لأن أهل بلدي يدرسون اللغة الفرنسية ولا يدرسون اللغة الانجليزية.

المدرس: في أي كلية تريد أن تدرس في العام المقبل يا مروان ؟

مروان: أريد أن أدرس في كلية الشريعة.

المدرس: في أي كلية تريد ان تدرس أنت يا موسى

(٤

عمرو : أرجوك أن تشتري لي هذا الكتاب من الهند عندما تذهب الى هناك في عطلة الصيف. انه باللغة الأردية. وما وجدته في المكتبات هنا

أيوب : أنا آسف. اني لن أذهب الى الهند في عطلة الصيف. أريد أن أذهب الى بغداد لأزور خالي الذي يعمل في سفارة الهند هناك

عمرو : واخوتك ، الا يذهبون الى الهند؟

أيوب : نعم، هم أيضا لن يذهبوا هذا العام. يريدون ان يبقوا بالمدينة المنورة ليحفظوا القرآن الكريم.

7. Explain any one of the following verses in English or Urdu or Hindi (15 marks)

(الف)

ورجا لي البرء السريع من السقم	قاس الحرارة جس نبضي بعدها
مرا ، ولكن فيه كشف للغمم	حضر الدواء فشربته فوجدته
فنشطت حتى من سروري لم أنم	فرحت لذا أمي وداعبني أبي
كذاك حب أبي فما هذي النعم	هذا حنان الأم من أجل ابنها
ومحبة ما شاء ربي ذو الكرم	لجزاء هذا الحب مني طاعة

(ب)

وأدفأه فانظر لقلة عقله	وجاء به يسعى الى الدار طائشا
وساحت سموم الموت في الجسم كله	فلما أحس الوحش بالدفء حوله
على الولد المسكين يبغي لقتله	وفتح عينيه وحرك رأسه
وداس عليه غاضبا بنعاله	أتاه أبوه عاجلا قط رأسه
ولا تصنع المعروف في غير أهله	وقال بني احذر لئيما لقيته

C.B.S.E MARCH 2006 Examination

1. Define and illustrate any two of the following terms with examples. (10 marks)

الفاعل ، مفعول فيه، اسم ان ،تثنية ، حروف جوازم الفعل المضارع ،
ضمير مجرور متصل

2. Translate any five of the following sentences into English or Urdu or Hindi (10 marks)

١) متى يعود أبوك من الهند؟

٢) هما طالبتان عاقلتان

٣) سمير أطول طالب في الفصل

٤) في جيبي مائة روبية

٥) أخي ما كتب الأجوبة على الكراسة

٦) مدرستي واقعة في المدينة الجديدة

٧) متى يسافر مدرسنا الى أمريكا ؟

٨) في أي بيت تسكن ؟

3. Translate any five of the following sentences into Arabic (10 marks)

1. Are you a student in this school?

2. Mohan and Sohan went to the railway station

3. They (women) have five hundred rupees.

4. They (men) are sleeping in the class room.

5. Verily Deepawali comes in October.

6. How is your friend?

7. Id comes after Ramazan.

8. The principal of our school is a very nice man.

4. Use any five of the following words in simple sentences (10 marks)

لم، ذاهبان، متى، حديقتان، ذاهبون، قالت، على، لن يفتح، كان، مائة

5. Write a short paragraph in Arabic on any one of the following topics. (10)

كلبي ، تاج محل ، سوق المدينة ، كرة القدم

6. Translate any two of the following passages into English, or Urdu or Hindi (35 marks)

١) علي: ادفترك هذا يا أحمد؟ ان خطك جميل جدا. ما شاء الله.

أحمد: شكرا يا علي. خطي جميل وخطك أجمل

علي: من هذا الفتى الذي معك يا أحمد ؟ كأنه أخوك

أحمد: نعم هو أخي الشقيق.

علي: أاكبر منك هو أو أصغر ؟

أحمد: هو أصغر مني.

علي: في أي مهجع انت يا أخي ؟

أحمد: أنا في المهجع الخامس. وهو بعيد جدا عن الجامعة.

علي: أنا في المهجع الثامن وهو أبعد من مهجعكم.

أحمد : أيهما أحسن ؟

علي: المهجع الخامس أحسن فان غرفه أوسع.

٢) ثم فتح المدرس كتابه وقرأ درسا جديدا : خلق الله الشمس والقمر والنجوم والأرض والبحار وخلق كل شيئ وخلق الانسان من طين... ثم قام وكتب هذا الدرس على السبورة.

رفع محمد يده وقال : ما معنى الطين يا أستاذ؟

المدرس : الطين معناه التراب المختلط بالماء

ورفع فيصل يده

فقال له المدرس: أعندك سؤال يا فيصل ؟

قال فيصل : نعم عندي سؤال. البحار جمع البحر.

قال المدرس: نعم هو كذلك. قام الحسن وقال ما جمع السماء يا أستاذ ؟

قال المدرس: جمعها سماوات

٣) عائشة: يا أبت انت اشتريت لي ملفا قبل اسبوع. اريد الآن ملفا آخر.

الأب. ماذا تريدين انت يا حفصة ؟

حفصة: أريد حقيبة

الأب: أما عندك حقيبة ؟

حفصة: بلى عندي حقيبة حمراء أريد حقيبة أخرى سوداء

الأب: ماذا تريدين يا سعاد؟

سعاد: عندي مسطرة صغيرة. أريد أخرى كبيرة.

الأب: وماذا تريدين انت يا ليلى؟

ليلى: أريد مصحفا ذا حرف كبير

الأب: أما تريدين شيئا يا سلمى ؟

سلمى: بلى أريد معجما انكليزيا وآخر فرنسيا.

7. Explain any one of the following verses in English or Urdu or Hindi (15 marks)

(الف)

وكلام أشخاص فوقعا بالقدم	حتى سمعت على السلام ضجة
هو ذا الطبيب لكي يعالجني قدم	هذا أبي وبجنبه رجل أتى
ورجا لي البرء السريع من السقم	قاس الحرارة جس نبضي بعدها
مرا ، ولكن فيه كشف للغمم	حضر الدواء فشربته فوجدته
فنشطت حتى من سروري لم أنم	فرحت لذا أمي وداعبني أبي

(ب)

لينقذوا غيرهم من العطب	يخاطرون بالنفوس في اللهب
وامرأة مسنة وكهل	كم أنقذوا من عاجز و طفل
ما صار لولاهم الى الضياع	وكم حموا من أنفس المتاع
عزمهم أمضى من النيران	فهم وان كانوا من الانسان
كما لهم جزائه الأسود	لهم حنان المشفق الودود

181

PORTIONS PRESCRIBED BY
C.B.S.E FOR STD: 9 and 10

ARABIC CODE NUMBER: 016
STD.9

Section: A

I. Grammar

1. Formation of Nominal Sentences (Mubtada and Khabar)
2. Formation of Maadi and all of its kinds
3. Formation of Simple Mudaare (Aorist)
4. Murakkab Jarri (Jarr and Majroor)
5. Murakkab Isharee (Ism Ishara and Musharun ilayhi)
6. Formation of Amr(Haazir, Ghaib and Mutakallim)
7. Formation of Nahi (Haazir, Ghaib and Mutakallim)
8. Formation of Ism Fael and Ism Mafool
9. Murakkab Wasfi (Mausof and Sifat)
10. Murakkab Izafee (Muzaf and Muzaaf Ilaih)

II. Translation

(1) Translation of simple sentences of Arabic into English Urdu or Hindi

(2) Translation of simple sentences of English, Urdu o Hindi into Arabic

III. Use of words in simple Arabic sentences.

Section: B

Prose And Poetry

Prose: Prescribed book: Duroosul Lughatil Arabiah Li ghairin Natiqeen Biha Part – 1 by Dr.V.Abdul Rahim

Poetry: Selected poems from Al-Qiraatur Rasheeda Part.1

Poems; Al-Mizyau, At-Tair, Tarnimatul Walad, Tarnimatul Umm, Al-Faer, Attaairu Wal-Banatu.

STD. 10

Section: A

. Grammar

1) Formation of verbal sentences (Fiel, Fael and Mafool Bihi)

2) Al Marfooaat

3) Al Mansoobat (Al Mafaeelul Khamsa, Ism inna wa akhawatuha, Khabar Kaana wa akhawatuha

4) Conjunctions (Huroof Atf)

5) Pronouns (Zamaer)

6) Dual (Tathniya)

7) Mudaare with huruf nawasib and jawazim

8) Jam'a salim and jam'a mukassar (Qillat and Kasrat)

9) Noon Khafeefah and Thaqeelah in Mudaare (Aorist)

I. Translation

(1) Translation of simple sentences of Arabic into English, Urdu or Hindi

(2) Translation of simple sentences of English, Urdu or Hindi into Arabic

III. Use of words in simple Arabic sentences.

IV: Composition (Short paragraph or letter on a given topic)

Section: B

Prose and Poetry

Prose: Prescribed book: Durroosul Lughatil Arabiah Lighairin Natiqeen Biha Part – 2 by Dr.V.Abdul Rahim

Poetry: Selected poems from Al Qiraaturrasheeda Part.2

Poems to be studied: An Nahla Wazzinbar, Wala Tasnael Ma'roof fi Ghairi Ahlihi, Jazaaul Walidain, Rijalul Mataafi